The Astrology of Rising Signs

CARL L SARGENT

The Astrology of Rising Signs

RIDER

London Melbourne Auckland Johannesburg

First published in 1986 in Great Britain by Rider & Co. Ltd,
an imprint of Century Hutchinson Ltd, Brookmount House,
62–65 Chandos Place, Covent Garden, London WC2N 4NW

Century Hutchinson Publishing Group (Australia) Pty Ltd
16–22 Church Street, Hawthorn, Melbourne, Victoria 3122

Century Hutchinson Group (NZ) Ltd
32–34 View Road. PO Box 40–086, Glenfield, Auckland 10

Century Hutchinson Group (SA) Pty Ltd
PO Box 337, Bergvlei 2012, South Africa

Typeset by Wyvern Typesetting Ltd, Bristol
Printed and bound in Great Britain by
Anchor Brendons Ltd, Tiptree, Essex

British Library Cataloguing in Publication Data
Sargent, Carl
The astrology of rising signs: how to
find your rising sign and its significance
for your whole life.
1. Astrology
I. Title
133.5   BF1708.1

ISBN 0–7126–1261–0

Contents

Contents

Preface

Most people know about 'sun signs' – the astrological signs you find described in newspapers and magazines. This book goes a little deeper – into Rising signs (and just what these are is explained completely in the pages which follow). To discover your Rising sign, you need to know where and (approximately) when you were born – and, despite the intimidating number of tables and stern-looking figures at the back of this book, only one single calculation taking about half a minute is needed. If you're wondering why such a simple business needs so many tables, they are simply there to provide necessary information for people born in all parts of the world, and not just in Britain.

This book is *not* a technical manual of astrology and the last thing I want to do is to blind you with arcane details and complicated calculations. You don't need any special knowledge or skills to understand and enjoy what you're about to read – and you're going to find it helpful and practically useful. Astrology is a useful part of human knowledge, there *is* 'something in it', and it can help people with their problems, relationships and everyday lives. And it can be fun reading a description of someone you know and checking how well it fits them! A friend of mine, a Leo, kindly read the section on Leo as a Rising sign – and he commented that while most of it was very accurate some parts were, well, maybe just a little bit less *flattering* than they should be. Which is, of course, *exactly* what you'd expect a Leo to say – for reasons you can find out shortly!

A final point: I use 'he' to stand for 'he' or 'she' throughout.

Have fun with this book, and I hope you're going to be able to put it to use too.

Carl Sargent
December 1985

Part One

YOUR RISING SIGN
AND WHAT IT MEANS

Your Sun sign

Opinion polls show that many people check their horoscopes every day in the newspaper. Knowing what 'sign' they are according to the day of their birth, they check the predictions given – 'What will today be like for money? Are there any tall dark handsome strangers on the horizon?'.

Such astrology is based on just one of the factors astrologers look at in a detailed horoscope, which can only be computed from knowing exactly where, and when (including the time of day), a person was born. This first factor is the *Sun sign*, and I'd better explain what that means.

To us on Earth, the Sun *appears* to travel around the earth, completing one full 'orbit' every year; it's this travelling which brings the progression of the seasons from winter to summer and back again. Actually, nothing of the sort really happens; it's the Earth, of course, which orbits around the Sun. But from *our* point of view it seems as if the Sun orbits round the Earth, and the path it seems to follow around us is called the *ecliptic*. That term you don't need to remember, but the important thing is this: around the ecliptic there is a narrow 'band' of constellations of stars, and these form the *Zodiac*. That's a term which most people do know; the Zodiac is divided into 12 'signs' by astrologers, and these are Aries, Taurus, Gemini . . . and on to the twelfth and last, Pisces. So, as the Sun 'moves' along the ecliptic in the 12 months of the year, it appears to be placed within one of these 12 signs, starting with Aries (in April) and then moving through Taurus, then Gemini and finally through to Pisces, then back into Aries as another springtime starts. Obviously, since the Sun spends 12 months completing a cycle of movement, and there are 12 Zodiac signs, it spends approximately one month in each sign. If you know the date of your birth, you will know your Sun sign; this is the Zodiac sign the Sun was 'located in' on the day you were born.

Most people do know what personality is associated with each sign by astrologers, but here I want to show the basic psychology of each one and do something more, which will be important later: the 12 Zodiac signs are linked into four sets of three, and if we look at the basic character of each sign we can begin to see why this is. The 12 Zodiac signs are:

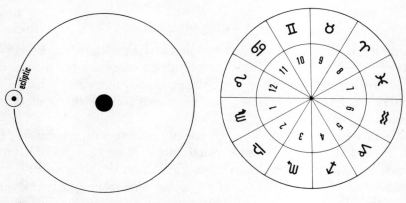

Zodiac sign	Basic psychological principle
1 Aries	Energy, aggression, physical force
2 Taurus	Practicality, steadiness
3 Gemini	Communicating, fast-thinking, versatility
4 Cancer	Emotion, moodiness, protectiveness
5 Leo	Pride, dignity, creativity
6 Virgo	Detailed thinking, analyzing things, coolness
7 Libra	Love of harmony, fairness, beauty; friendships
8 Scorpio	Power, secretiveness, charisma, personal 'magnetism'
9 Sagittarius	Generosity, enthusiasm, restlessness, ingenuity
10 Capricorn	Caution, practicality, 'building'
11 Aquarius	Rebelliousness, ingenuity, sociability
12 Pisces	Compassion, dreaminess, restlessness

You will notice that all I'm giving here is a short list of words which describe the basic psychology of each sign. You can't give a complete picture of a person from knowing the Sun sign alone, because there are so many other factors which are important in the full horoscope. You're better off thinking in terms simply of the basics for each of the 12 signs.

You may also notice that the 12 are not completely independent of each other – it would be surprising if they were! The 12 signs can be grouped into four sets of three, each of them associated by astrologers with one of the old Elements from which the world was formed in legend. These are:

Fire: Aries, Leo, Sagittarius (1st, 5th, 9th)
Earth: Taurus, Virgo, Capricorn (2nd, 6th, 10th)
Air: Gemini, Libra, Aquarius (3rd, 7th, 11th)
Water: Cancer, Scorpio, Pisces (4th, 8th, 12th)

The important point is that each of these four elements is also associated with a basic psychological force within us – and, looking at the four sets of signs, we can begin to see what this is for each element and why the signs are linked with each other.

Some of the groups of three fit together obviously – look at the three Earth signs. The basic Earth quality of being practical (but rather unimaginative) and creating things comes across clearly for all the three signs there. The emotion of the Water signs is clear too. Perhaps Libra doesn't seem to fit so obviously with Gemini and Aquarius – but it does when you think about it; the 'reasoning' of Air can be seen in the way Libra likes to get his or her friends to agree on things and be happy with each other. Libra instinctively knows how to balance people and their interests; this isn't usually done in a calculating, thinking way, it's instinctive, but Libra goes about it in a straightforward way which shows that the rational power of Air is in this sign. And Libra has the light, friendly, Airy quality too. And, lastly, the Fire signs all fit, their energies moving in different ways – for Aries the fiery nature is obvious, Leo has the pride and creativity of Fire and Sagittarius the restless side of Fire (the flames leap and crackle with this sign) and the enthusiasm too.

Now, why does this matter? There are two major reasons. The first is that, as you can see, the 12 signs aren't quite independent and some of them have features in common (some are opposed, too – Fire and Water will never mix). This matters because, when we discover what the Rising sign – as opposed to the Sun sign – actually is and what we can learn from it, how the influences of different signs affect each other will be important. What we shall see is that certain typical patterns of byplay between them crop up again and again – which is because groups of them (the threes) have certain features in common. You'll see how this works in Part 2 of this

FIRE Passion, strong energy, the urge to do things and achieve things	*Aries* Physical energy, willpower *Leo* Creativity, pride in achievements *Sagittarius* Restless mental energy, ideas and ideals expressing these
WATER Emotional sensitivity, feeling, intuition	*Cancer* Moodiness, emotional sensitivity, protectiveness, 'mothering' *Scorpio* Emotional power, charisma, 'deep' awareness *Pisces* Dreaminess, compassion, unselfishness, intuition
AIR The power of reason, but also a highly sociable element	*Gemini* Versatility, mental speed, fast thinking – fast talking *Libra* Friendliness, grace, love of harmony, balancing people and feelings *Aquarius* Ingenious thinking, inventiveness, rebelliousness, friendliness
EARTH The practical, constructive ability to get things done – but lacks imagination and is rarely highly intelligent	*Taurus* Steadiness, practicality, conventiality, love of beauty *Virgo* Attention to detail, prudence, coolness, 'checking the small print' *Capricorn* Building things, career responsibility, duty

book, and from seeing the grouping of the signs now, you'll have an idea of just *why* we find patterns recurring when we get into more detail on Rising signs.

The other reason is simple – in the last Part of this book we'll be looking at Sun signs and Rising signs together. There are 144 possible combinations of these, and it's impossible to describe all of them! It's much easier if we can consider them in groups – and that can be done if we take them according to their grouping under the four elements. But that's for later, and now we want to consider another question. We know what a Sun sign is, but we don't yet know what a Rising sign is. We're going to see that the Rising sign is more important than the Sun sign, and gives an astrologer a lot more information about someone's personality. So just what is it, and how can you find out what your Rising sign is?

The Rising sign
and what it means

The Sun sign, to recap, is the Zodiac sign the Sun 'occupies' on the day of your birth. It changes about once a month, since it takes 12 months to travel through the Zodiac (from our point of view) and there are 12 signs.

The Rising sign changes every day – indeed, 12 times a day. The Earth orbits round the Sun, but it also spins on its own axis every 24 hours – which brings the progression of night and day. As the Earth rotates, the Zodiac sign which is 'rising' over the horizon changes. If this puzzles you, think of it this way: on any given day, the Sun stays more or less fixed in one Zodiac sign. But, of course, the Sun rises in the morning, reaches its zenith at noon, and then sets in the evening (we can do without the complications of everlasting nights at the Arctic at this stage!). So, clearly, the Zodiac sign it's in will also 'rise' over the horizon in the morning, just as the Sun does, and 'set' at night. The Rising sign is the Zodiac sign which is rising over the eastern horizon (where the Sun rises) at the moment of your birth – actually, the definition is more technical than this, but this will do for now. Obviously, this sign is going to change rapidly; because the Earth rotates once a day, the Rising sign will change, moving through all 12 signs in 24 hours. So the Rising sign changes every two hours or so, as opposed to the Sun sign which changes only once a month. So, to know your Rising sign, you need to know approximately when you were born, at least within an hour or so (and where, but that's presumably no problem). This is easy for people in many countries where the authorities request the birth time to be put on the birth certificate but in Britain, alas, this is not done. However, it's surprising how many parents recall the time of birth of their children with great accuracy. Well, maybe it isn't so surprising; giving birth isn't an experience mothers tend to forget and fathers may recall the time they were able to stop pacing the corridors of the maternity hospital because they received the glad news!

So we know what the Rising sign is, and later we shall look at how to work out what it is, given the time and place of birth. The obvious question is, why bother? What can the Rising sign tell us about someone that a Sun sign cannot? The answer is, a great deal, but we need one last technical detail before we can see why this is so.

In constructing a full horoscope, astrologers represent the positions of the Sun, Moon and planets within a full circle – the 360° 'wheel' of the Zodiac. And this wheel is divided into twelve equal segments, called *houses*. Each of these houses is argued by astrologers to govern a particular area of a person's life, and we shall shortly see what the influences of the houses are. Our starting point is this: the Rising sign is the sign which 'rules' the first house, and once we know what this is, we know the signs which rule all the other 11. If Aries rules the first house, Taurus rules the second, Gemini the third, and so on; likewise if Capricorn rules the first, Aquarius rules the second, Pisces the third, and so on.

This may be getting confusing, and since this isn't a technical manual of astrology here's a way of thinking about what's going on: consider the horoscope wheel and the 12 houses, as the face of a clock. The houses – just like the figures on a clock face – stay put. What moves around the clock, of course, are the hands; and the Zodiac signs, changing as the Earth spins, are like the hands on this clock face (a 24-hour clock, to be precise). If, at one particular time and place, Gemini is the Rising sign and thus Cancer rules the second house and Leo the third and so on, two hours later this will have moved on; now Cancer will rule the first house (being the Rising sign), Leo the second, Virgo the third, and so on. If these technicalities still puzzle you, it doesn't matter too much; you can still work out your Rising sign and read about what it means for you. There's one last point to clear up; the point that signs 'rule' houses. What this means, for someone's personality, is that the personality traits of the sign linked with the house in question will come into play most strongly when the affairs in life connected with that house are involved. One example: for a person with Taurus rising, the sign Gemini will 'rule' the second house, and this house is concerned primarily with money matters. Since Gemini is versatile, clever and communicates itself well, this tells us that many Taurus people can be wise in their money dealings and their dealings with others will be profitable because they can use Gemini's persuading talents to convince others that they're trustworthy with money. The versatile side of Gemini makes the person with Taurus rising particularly creative with money – they may have several sources of income. Now, this is somewhat unusual for Taurus people in terms of their general psychology because, frankly, this isn't a particularly bright sign. But when it comes to money, that's another matter.

This one example is starting to show us why knowing about the Rising sign can be very informative. You don't just learn about one factor – but about 12, because the other 11 signs ruling the other 11 houses also tell us something about a person. The Sun sign tells us one thing about a person, but the Rising sign tells us 12 things. We'll now look at the 12 houses and the spheres of life they're associated with, but two points first. The first point is that the 12 houses aren't the same as the 12 signs. The signs are personality characteristics, influences, *styles* of thinking, feeling and doing things. The houses concern areas of life, specific and concrete events and possibilities. But they are linked. The sphere of life governed by the fourth house, for example, is home life: a person's home base and his feelings about it (does he need one or is he a wanderer?) and his family life. The fourth *sign* is Cancer, and this is well known as a motherly, protective sign, compassionate and caring. So we can see fairly clearly that there is a link between the fourth house and the fourth sign; the area of life the house is connected with and the psychology of the sign have something in common.

The second point is this: the first house, the one ruled by the Rising sign, tells us about the *general* personality of a person, the typical ways in which they think, feel and react. This influence extends to *all* areas of life, and we can think of the Rising sign determining a person's *overlay* of personality, a general influence affecting everything. The other 11 signs, ruling the other 11 houses, affect more specific areas of life, and if we want to understand how a person handles money, his career, education, emotions and relationships, we look at how the *general* personality overlay (Rising sign) interacts with the *specific* influence of the sign ruling the house connected with money, romance, the home, and so on. Let's go back to our person with Taurus rising to see how this works. We've seen that Gemini ruling his second house makes him imaginative and clever in money dealings, and to this Gemini influence we can add Taurus' *general* personality, which is a careful, practical one. So, with his money Taurus will be imaginative and intelligent but also careful; his balance of caution with speculation is just about right. But Taurus can bring a weakness, because Taurus likes a bit of self-indulgence now and then and he can overspend on luxuries for himself . . . we can begin to see how the *general* influence of Taurus (which affects everything) and the *specific* influence of Gemini (which, ruling the second house, influences primarily money affairs) can be put together to give a detailed picture of how someone with Taurus rising handles money. As we look through all the interplays of the Rising sign and the other 11 for each Rising sign, we begin to see why certain people have strengths and weaknesses, particular areas of ease and conflict, within themselves. So far as Taurus and his money goes, the Gemini influence on money is pretty good. It gives him a bit of flair he might otherwise lack and there's not much conflict there. But someone with Sagittarius rising (Sagittarius loves impulse spending) has Capricorn (very practical, careful, wants to save money) ruling the second house and that's a conflict if ever there was one! But enough examples. Let's look at the 12 houses in more detail, and the areas of life connected with them.

1st House This is the house 'ruled' by the Rising sign, and the general personality of an individual is influenced by this sign, as we've seen.

2nd House This house is linked with money and financial affairs; money planning, investments, and spending the stuff.

3rd House This house is associated with communicating; the styles of expression people use, their manners and mannerisms, how they talk, write and generally convey their ideas to others.

4th House This house is linked with the home, both as a physical place one lives in, and also with family life, one's attitudes to parents and children.

5th House This house is concerned with creativity, and also with romance and sexuality. By 'creativity' I mean the urge to do things which give someone a feeling of real accomplishment, rather than routine work.

6th House   This house is concerned with work, especially practical work and work where attention to detail is important. Also with service; how people are useful to, and help, others.

7th House   This house is often known as the house of marriage, but close partnerships of any kind – notably business ones – are involved here too.

8th House   This house is associated with how we express our needs to other people, and how they react to us; these are usually material and practical needs but sometimes emotional ones too.

9th House   We can think of this as the house of 'far horizons'; how people want to grow, to learn new things and wander far and free in their imaginations and even in the real world, through travel.

10th House   The house of career, how ambitious we are and how we arrange our career lives, the people who can help us with career, and career prospects.

11th House   The house of friendships and acquaintances, more superficial than the 7th house partnerships.

12th House   The house of hidden things, the Unconscious mind, the part of us we find most difficult to recognize, understand, or develop. Sometimes, inner weaknesses or possible fated ill-luck may be linked with the 12th house.

First, we can see that the affairs of life linked with these 12 houses are not completely different. For example, if we want to know details of how someone gets on at work we would look at the 10th house (career) but obviously the 6th house (work in a more general sense) is involved too. And if we wanted to think about how someone got on with other people at work, the 11th, 3rd, and perhaps the 7th and 8th houses would come into the picture too. Astrology reflects the complexity of our lives; in our careers, we deal with the work we do, money affairs, the people we meet, our regular work-mates and helpers – even doing work at home. Different houses in the horoscope tell us about these different areas of our lives, and about our probable strengths and weaknesses in different ways.

Also, as you've probably seen, the houses and signs do indeed have some correspondence with each other. As an example, the 9th house of 'far horizons' has much in common with the ninth sign,

Sagittarius, a notoriously restless and imaginative sign. As another, the 12th house is concerned with the unconscious mind and 'hidden' parts of personality. Likewise the twelfth sign, Pisces, is a dreaming sign, inspired by ideas and images welling up from the Unconscious, intuitive and sensitive but finding it very hard to express these ideas in words – a prime function of the developed conscious mind, but one the Unconscious has a lot of trouble with.

Finally, you may be wondering where this leaves the Sun sign. What is there left for the Sun sign to tell us, if the Rising sign can tell us so much about someone? The Rising sign tells us much about the general, superficial personality of the person, their typical ways of thinking, feeling and reacting, and the signs ruling the other 11 houses tell us details about specific areas of their lives and personalities. What the Sun sign tells us is much less than newspaper astrologers would have us believe: it tells us something (but not everything) about what is most deeply important to someone. It does not, I think, tell us very much about someone's day-to-day life and how others see them. The affairs linked with the Sun sign are those which a person cherishes deep down, but may not affect him much for 99% of his waking life. The Rising sign is much more likely to tell us about someone's typical life and general personality. And, to finish off with, the Rising sign can also tell us about the emotional 'heart' of someone when we know the house which is ruled by the sign Leo. I shall call this the 'Leo factor'; Leo is the sign associated with our creativity, and when Leo's influence is felt in our lives, we can achieve the things we most want to and feel the deepest sense of satisfaction. As an example, for a person with Libra as the Rising sign (or Libra rising, if you prefer), Leo rules the 11th house of friendships. Librans are intensely sociable people, and generally greatly dislike being alone. So they should, since Leo's rulership of the 11th tells us that they feel most creative when there are other people around them. And another strange, quirky little observation I've made can be explained by this Leo factor: I have often been asked by people to guess their Sun sign, which many people interested in astrology get asked to do (and usually hate, since it reduces astrology to a parlour game and it really *is* a more serious business than this). I'm not right very often, but I have found that I can recognize people with Gemini or Sagittarius rising particularly easily; they do stick out a mile. There's a good reason for this; these two we can call 'perfect' signs (which Geminis and

Sagittarians will like because neither is averse to being flattered), because for Gemini rising, Leo rules the third house (and Gemini is the third sign in the Zodiac) and for Sagittarius rising Leo rules the ninth (and likewise Sagittarius is the ninth Zodiac sign). What this means is that in both cases the general personality 'overlay' of the person, and the most powerful force within them (the Leo factor), have a great deal in common. Geminis and Sagittarians are indeed exactly what they appear to be, and their 'superficial' personalities are in perfect harmony with their deeper drives and instincts. Other examples of how the 'Leo factor' works in astrology can be found in the later chapters describing the individual Rising signs.

This isn't to say that the Sun sign can be entirely ignored, though, and knowing both the Rising sign and the Sun sign can tell us more than either alone. How combinations affect personal psychology is the subject for Part 3 of this book – but now, we can deal with how to work out your Rising sign.

FINDING OUT YOUR RISING SIGN

You need to know two things to compute your Rising sign; where you were born, and the time and date

The *time* you should try to find out as exactly as possible. Sometimes, an error of a few minutes can be crucial, but sometimes even an hour or so makes no difference. However, when you finish working out your Rising sign, you will know whether an error of a few minutes might be important or not.

The *place* you should presumably know! However, ideally you should find out the *longitude* and *latitude* of your birthplace from an atlas. If you don't have ready access to an atlas, or you want to take a short-cut, in Table 1 at the back of the book there is a lengthy list of major cities around the world with their longitudes and latitudes given. For people unfamiliar with these terms, *latitude* is how far north (or south) a place is from the equator. Likewise, *longitude* is how far east (or west) a place is from a 'line' drawn between the North and South poles (and passing through Greenwich, London, on the way).

For British readers, the longitude of their place of birth isn't crucially important, although if you want to be precise about working out your Rising sign then it is important to check this. The computation of the Rising sign is much easier for readers born in

Britain than for those elsewhere, because of time differences between different countries, as we shall soon see. So, we'll begin here with an example of how to work out the Rising sign for a British birth, and then go through the more complicated case of a birth outside the UK.

Rising signs: British births

You need to know the place, date and time of your birth. Let's take as an example someone born in the exotic English town of Milton Keynes at 5.15 in the morning on 17 July 1970 (the year does not matter in the calculations we're about to go through).

First, from Table 4 in the back of this book we need to look up what is known as *Sidereal Time* on the day in question. Sidereal Time is the time scale used in Zodiacal and astrological computations, and it is not the same as clock time. Table 4 tells us the Sidereal Time at Greenwich, London, at *noon*, and if we check the table we see that for 17 July this was 07.41 hours.

The next thing we need to do is to adjust this time for the difference between noon and the time of birth. The birth occurred 6 hours and 45 minutes *before* noon; and so we have to subtract 6 hours and 45 minutes from the 07.41 figure. This leaves us with the figure of 00.56. (Now, if this birth had been an hour earlier we would have come up with a *negative* figure: minus 4 minutes! This can happen in computation, and to correct for it simply *add* 24 hours to any negative figure you get (this would give 23.56 here). Likewise, you can get a figure exceeding 24 hours, and when this happens just knock off 24 hours from the figure you get.)

Let's recap on what we're doing: we are converting 'clock time' into a special form of time, known as Sidereal Time, which is the basis of astrologers' computations. In the example above, we have read off from Table 4 in this book the Sidereal Time at *noon* (going by 'clock time') and, to work out the Sidereal Time when this person was born, we correct for the difference between noon and the birth time. Since the birth was *before* noon, we *subtract* that difference from the noontime Sidereal Time. If the birth had been later than noon, we would have added the difference: a birth at 4.40 in the afternoon on that same day would have taken place at a Sidereal Time of (07.41 + 04.40 =) 12.21. All we have to do now is to read one figure off from Table 5.

The one last thing we need to know to use Table 5 is the *latitude* of the place of birth – Milton Keynes. To work out the Rising sign quickly, we know that Milton Keynes is fairly close to London, and that London is 51½ degrees (or 51½°) north of the equator. Table 5 gives us times for when different Rising signs 'rise' over the eastern horizon at different latitudes (this is not exactly technically correct, but it is easier to grasp what's going on if I put it this way). These times are Sidereal Times – hence our need to convert normal 'clock time' for a birth into Sidereal Time previously. And the table gives times for different latitudes from 2° to 60° north of the equator in 2° intervals. The closest table for London (or Milton Keynes) is the 52° table. We know the Sidereal Time at the moment of birth: 00.56. What we see from Table 5 is that, at this latitude, the sign Leo 'rises' at 00.17 and the sign Virgo rises later, at 03.08. Since 00.56 is later than the time Leo rises, but earlier than the time that Virgo rises, the Rising sign here is Leo. And, finally, since we have worked out a birth time (in Sidereal Time) 29 minutes later than when Leo started to rise, we know that an error of 29 minutes or so in the birth time would make no difference to things. As long as this person feels certain that they know their birth time within 20 minutes or so, Leo is definitely the Rising sign. But if they didn't know for sure – and it could have been an hour or so either way – then we *cannot* be absolutely sure that Leo is the Rising sign, although it probably would be (it would certainly be either Leo or the sign Cancer; an hour *later* would still leave the Rising sign in Leo, but an hour earlier would place it in Cancer). The solution to this problem is either to badger your parents or other possibly knowledgeable people until you get a reasonably accurate birth time, or else to read the descriptions for both Cancer and Leo (in the example we have here) and see which fits you best. They are rather different signs and the odds are you'll recognize which one is the correct one. Having determined Leo as the rising sign, all you need to do is to move on to Part 2 and start reading about this sign . . .

. . . with one last warning. Like many countries, Britain keeps Summer Time at irregular dates (and, for people born during World War II, Double Summer Time in some years). Helpfully, in Table 3 there is a list of British Summer Time for years in this century. If you were born on a day when Summer Time was in operation, always subtract 1 hour (2 hours for Double Summer Time) from your birth time before working out the Sidereal Time.

Rising signs: births outside the UK

A first word of warning – if you skipped the last section on UK births, please go back and read it. The logic of what's going on in working out Rising signs is covered there, and here we need to add extra complications to it!

The major complication arising for births outside the UK is this: there are time differences between the UK and countries abroad, and indeed within some large countries (Canada, America and Australia for example) there are different time zones within a single country. Countries lying *east* of Britain have their local time *ahead* of London and those lying *west* have their local time *behind* London. To take two examples, New York is five hours behind London and Melbourne 10 hours ahead; so when it is noon in London (ignoring the complications of Summer Time) it is 7 a.m. (07.00) in New York and 10.00 p.m. (22.00) in Melbourne. There are also differences involved in working out Rising signs for people born in Northern and Southern hemispheres, so as a first example we deal with a Northern hemisphere birth. However, all the steps involved here are also involved in working out a Rising sign for a Southern hemisphere birth.

The first step is to find out the clock time in London when the person was born – the birth time in Greenwich (London) Mean Time (GMT) for the birth. To compute this, you will need to know the time difference between your country of birth and Britain. In Table 2 at the back of the book, there is a long listing of such time differences; if your country isn't listed then you may need to check with an official statistical source what this time difference is (telephone companies can also be helpful). You will also need to check whether Summer Time was in effect when you were born.

If Summer Time was in operation when you were born – and it's impossible to list all Summer Time variations for different countries in this book – *always* subtract this from your time of birth before proceeding with the next step in working out your Rising sign.

Now, if your country of birth was *east* of Britain, you should *subtract* the time difference from your local time of birth; if it was *west, add* that difference. Let us look at an example; someone born in New York on 17 October 1958 (the year, in fact, doesn't matter), at 1.40 in the afternoon (13.40). New York time is five hours 'behind' London time (GMT), so we *add* five hours to the New

York time of birth. This gives us the figure 18.40, which is GMT for the time of birth.

The second step is to convert this GMT into Sidereal Time, a time scale used by astrologers. First, we shall compute London Sidereal Time. To do this, we simply look up Table 4, and check the time given against the date, 17 October. This time is 13.43. This is the Sidereal Time at *noon* GMT on 17 October. But, of course, this birth did not take place at noon GMT – it took place at 18.40 GMT. Since it took place *later* than noon, we *add* the difference between noon (12.00) and this figure (18.40), which is 6 hours and 40 minutes, to the Sidereal Time of 13.43 – giving us a value of 20.23 hours. This is the Sidereal Time in London when this New York birth took place.

(At this stage, note that you can get figures above 24 hours or below zero – if our birth in the example above had taken place four hours later, we would have the figure 24.23 for London Sidereal Time. If this happens, don't worry. If the London Sidereal Time is greater than 24 hours, just knock 24 hours off. If it is below zero, simply add 24 hours to it. In this way, you will end up with a figure between 00.01 and 24.00 hours.)

Now, we know the Sidereal Time in London when this person was born – 20.23. But this isn't what we need to know, although it's a step on the way; we need to know the Sidereal Time in *New York* when this person was born. This is the last step in our calculation, and for this we need to know the *longitude* of New York. From an atlas (or from Table 1 at the back of this book) we find that this is 74° west of London. We need to convert this longitude into a time correction, using the formula: 1° of longitude = 4 minutes of time. Since New York is *west* of London, we *subtract* the longitude/time factor from the London Sidereal Time. The time equivalent (if you like) of 74° is 296 minutes, or 4 hours and 56 minutes. Subtracting 04.56 from 20.23, we are left with the time: 15.27. This is the Sidereal Time in New York when the person was born – we can call this *local* Sidereal Time.

All we have to do now is to consult Table 5 to check the Rising sign. To do this, we need to know the *latitude* of New York, and again from an atlas we can find that this is slightly under 41° north of the equator. Using the 40° latitude column in Table 5, we find that the sign Aquarius begins to rise at 15.20 and Pisces at 16.50 (Sidereal Times) – so this person is born with Aquarius rising.

However, the error margin here is only 7 minutes – an error of greater than this *could* put this person into Capricorn rising. Fortunately, since birth times are recorded on American birth certificates, the error should be less than this so far as the birth time record goes. It might, however, be worth your time, if the error margin in computing your birth time is as narrow as this, to use the precise, detailed method given in the final section of this chapter.

(A point which may have occurred to more technically-minded readers is that, in the computation above, we are making two time corrections – one for local time differences and one for longitude differences from London. These are in opposite directions: the correction for time zone differences was an *addition* to London time, the longitude/time equivalence factor was *subtracted* from it. What's more, the times involved – 5 hours, and 4 minutes 56 seconds – were almost exactly the same. So why bother? Why not ignore these complications if they cancel out? The answer is that they don't always cancel out, exactly. Time zones are crude; they can cover large areas of territory and we shall see, in our next example, that an error of 20–30 minutes can be introduced if we simply ignore time zone and longitude corrections. As we've already seen in our New York example, such an error could lead to a complete mistake in identifying someone's Rising sign.)

Let's summarize our New York example, and the procedure followed.

(1) Correct the birth time for time zone difference from London (GMT), including a correction for local Summer Time if needed. If the birth place is *west* of London, *add* the difference to the birth time; if it is *east*, *subtract* the difference.

(2) Find the London Sidereal Time at the moment of birth. To do this, use Table 4. This table gives *noon* GMT Sidereal Times for each date in the year; obviously, correct the Sidereal Time for the difference from noon GMT at the time of birth (for an 07.00 GMT birth, for example, subtract 5 hours from the noontime Sidereal Time given in Table 4).

(3) Now find the local Sidereal Time at birth – that is, the Sidereal Time at the birthplace when the person was born. To do this, you need to know the *longitude* of the birthplace, and convert this into a time factor using the equation 1° of longitude = 4 minutes of time. If

the birthplace lies *west* of London, *subtract* this time factor from the London Sidereal Time at birth; if it lies *east* of London, *add* it.

(4) To read off the Rising sign, use Table 5: for this, you need to know the *latitude* of the birthplace to the nearest 2° (the table is spaced in 2° intervals). Knowing the local Sidereal Time at birth, just read off down the appropriate latitude column. The time listed opposite each sign is the Sidereal Time when the sign 'starts rising over the horizon'. From this time, and the time when later signs start to rise, you can easily discover what the Rising sign is for any birth time at a given latitude.

This formula works for any birth in the Northern hemisphere. For Southern hemisphere births, matters are a little more complicated. All the steps in the above calculation are needed, and two others also. As an example, we shall use a birth in Melbourne, Australia, at 9.20 p.m. on 26 November 1977 (again, the year doesn't matter).

The first step is to convert the birth time into GMT. Melbourne local time is 10 hours ahead of GMT, so GMT for the birth is 21.20 less 10 hours; 11.20 GMT. Noon Sidereal Time in London on 26 November is 16.21; since the birth occurred 40 minutes before noon, London Sidereal Time for the birth was 15.41.

Melbourne lies east of London – a long way east since it lies 145°E in longitude terms. The time correction we need is thus 145 × 4 minutes, 580 minutes, or 9 hours and 40 minutes. Since Melbourne lies east of London, we add this time factor to the London Sidereal Time to get local Sidereal Time; we get the figure 25.21, so we subtract 24 hours from that and we are left with 01.21.

All these steps are the same as for a Northern hemisphere example. Now there are two additional steps. The first is that *we add 12 hours to this birth time*. This gives us the figure 13.21. We now read off this time on Table 5, using the right latitude for Melbourne – this is 38° S, so we use the 38° column. There, we find that the sign Capricorn rises at 13.19 and Aquarius at 15.15, so a birth time of 13.21 just places this person under Capricorn.

But what we now do is to *reverse* this sign; the correct Rising sign, for a Southern hemisphere birth, is the *opposite* Zodiac sign to the one we read off from Table 5. The rule is:

For Aries read Libra and vice versa
For Taurus read Scorpio and vice versa
For Gemini read Sagittarius and vice versa
For Cancer read Capricorn and vice versa
For Leo read Aquarius and vice versa
For Virgo read Pisces and vice versa

Thus our Melbourne birth is under the sign Cancer. The 12-hour addition and sign-reversal isn't some fudge factor used by astrologers; there are technical reasons for this, but again, I won't go into these here.

Now, in this Melbourne example a possible error of just a few minutes would change the Rising sign we calculated. And some readers may need precise, technical computations of their Rising signs in which errors of just 1–2 minutes may be vital. The next section gives details of ultra-precise calculations – readers who don't need them can skip this section!

Rising signs – precise measurements

(1) *Sidereal Times*   As a matter of fact, Sidereal Times change slightly from year to year, and the data given in Table 4 in this book come from a computer-averaging of data between the 1930s and late 1970s. The maximum error which could arise from using this table is around four minutes, and for the large majority of cases the error will be less than two minutes or so. To obtain a precise Sidereal Time, you will need an *Emphemeris* for the year of your birth. These are available from the publisher W. Foulsham & Co. Ltd, Yeovil Road, Slough SL1 4JH, United Kingdom; write and enquire about price and availability. This publisher will supply foreign customers. An important technical note is that in relatively recent years, Sidereal Time in the Ephemeris has been given in Ephemeris time and not in GMT equivalent, and although the difference is usually around 1 minute or so, it is worth correcting for this. The Ephemeris always gives details of Ephemeris Time and GMT and their difference.

(2) *Exact longitudes and latitudes*   In Table 1, longitudes and latitudes are given to the nearest degree. For longitude, the maximum error this could introduce into a calculation is only 2 minutes (since 1° = 4 minutes in the conversion, and the maximum error is 2

minutes from a 'rounding-up' from half a degree). It may be worthwhile consulting an atlas to get minutes and degrees of longitude, given in the form X° Y'. One minute of longitude will equal 4 seconds of time, since there are 60 minutes of longitude in one degree.

Exact latitude may be worth discovering from an atlas, and then interpolating into Table 5. Table 5 gives rising times for signs at 2° latitude intervals, but one can fairly easily work out finer detail from the tables. For example, if Sagittarius rises at 08.21 at 32°, 08.23 at 34° and 08.25 at 36° one can very easily work out that it rises at 08.22 at 33° and 08.24 at 35°. Actually, except at moderately extreme latitudes, precise calculation will not add greatly to the exactitude of your working out of the Rising sign – but it is always worth being precise if a few minutes either way could make all the difference.

These precision-adjustments are probably worth making if (1) you know that a small time difference could change the Rising sign *and* (2) you can be certain that your time of birth was accurately recorded. There's little point in getting two or three extra minutes in precision from longitude and latitude corrections if you know that your information about your birth time is rather vague. Under such circumstances, work out your Rising sign and read both the description for that sign *and* the other possible sign (unless the possible error is very great, there should only be one possible alternative). You should be able to tell which is the correct one!

SO WHAT DOES THE RISING SIGN REALLY TELL YOU?

I've already explained what, in terms of astrology, the Rising sign can tell you about yourself and how this differs from the Sun signs you read about in your newspapers and the like. There are two final points to make before – knowing your Rising sign as you do by now (hopefully) – you turn over and read about it in Parts 2 and 3. The first is this: the Rising sign can tell you about strengths and weaknesses in your personality *and* pinpoint the root of certain conflicts in many cases. What's more, information from the Rising sign and the signs ruling the other 11 houses of the horoscope can pinpoint how to deal with those conflicts. *This information is useful, practical.*

The other point is this: just because astrology is useful, and it works, this does not mean that everything is fixed, predictable from astrology, and that people have no free will, or anything like this. If there is a neat way of summing up astrology it's this: it is a body of knowledge which can help you to swim with the tide in your life, by telling you about the easier and more productive ways of doing things, interacting with other people and solving problems. If you choose not to swim with the tide and play to your strengths, that's up to you: you can choose to deal with things the hard way. But if you do want to learn how knowing about Rising signs help, turn over and begin reading.

Part Two

THE 12 RISING SIGNS
ARIES TO PISCES

Aries rising
THE RAM

This ram is the leader of the flock. Powerful and aggressive, Aries takes second place to no-one. Aries dominates through the sheer force of his will, and it's active domination; Aries subjugates others and rules over them. Leo may be the king within the Zodiac, but Aries would then surely be the military general who *really* holds the power in the kingdom. Let the monarch step out of line and there will be a swift (and possibly bloody) military coup.

This sounds harsh and almost cruel. Indeed, Aries is abrasive and not bursting with compassion, but he is a great creator. Aries invents, creates, initiates projects and gets things done. His tremendous energies are indeed directed at increasing his own repute and strengthening his powerful ego but most other people benefit in the process. Aries does not waste time, and he is driven to competitiveness and excellence. He is, in fact, very self-critical, and even being number one is hardly enough for him. It must have been an Aries who, in the old joke, storms through the gates of heaven on Judgement Day and demands to know of God what *he's* doing on that throne.

Obviously, with Aries ruling the first house, every later house is ruled by its 'natural' sign. This might suggest a perfect state of affairs, but this isn't always so, because all the specific influences of the other signs on the other 11 houses must interact with the general personality of Aries. Sometimes, this can create conflicts.

Aries' general personality overlay is that of aggression, endeavour and sheer willpower. This is the most forceful sign in the Zodiac.

SECOND HOUSE (MONEY)
Ruler Taurus

Aries wants money just as he wants everything else in life. Taurus ruling the second house gives him the practical gifts to do this; Aries will see opportunities and seize them.

The negative side is that, while Taurus doesn't cheat, both Taurus and Aries are rather fixed and unchangeable in their approaches. Aries may be so determined to force through some project or other he's got his heart and head fixed on that he can court financial disaster through sheer stubbornness. To admit that some project is a failure and should be jacked in is an admission of personal failure to Aries. This is not to be countenanced. Aries can persist with projects when everyone else can see that they are doomed. It is wise for Aries not to put all his eggs in one basket. When he has an investment portfolio (which he probably will) investments should be spread around. A carefully calculated percentage of his capital (Taurus can figure out such things) can be used for risky investments.

The other major problem for Aries is wasting money on luxuries. Taurus likes this, and for Aries it's a way of showing off his wealth to others and proving how good he is at collecting wealth. Again, Aries should work out what he can afford on such things and how much is going too far.

THIRD HOUSE (COMMUNICATING)
Ruler Gemini

With Gemini ruling the third house and Sagittarius ruling the ninth, Aries has no shortage of ideas. He can be inspired (Sagittarius) and very clever at getting across to other people (Gemini). He has great conversational skills and he writes well. He is clear, concise and potentially a good persuader.

The problem is Aries' forcefulness. If he can hold back just a little, the Gemini skills can get him what he wants because other people respect his talents. But Aries always wants to *demand* things. What he has to learn is where he can demand and where he needs to persuade. Who will happily take his more aggressive side, and who will be annoyed by it and turn away? Aries must check this carefully.

Aries also wants to be known for his cleverness (Gemini is not averse to a little flattery and Aries always wants it). Flattering Arians on their force of argument is always a wise move, and Aries responds well to anyone suggesting new ways of developing arguments or new ways of getting the message across (Gemini's versatility again). And Aries is also a storehouse of information. The Gemini side, with Aries' willpower, wants to know everything. Aries has a good memory and cultivating his friendship can be worth it not least for what you can learn from him!

FOURTH HOUSE (HOME)
Ruler Cancer

Cancer does make Aries emotionally attached to his home, but in typical Aries style it's the hard shell of the crab which may be the more obvious aspect of Cancer's influence. Aries is fiercely proud of his home. He loves his family and any insult to a family member will provoke Aries' rage (which is pretty unpleasant). There's a good reason for this. Aries needs his home to feel emotionally secure. Any threat to his home is a threat to his well-being; you have found the crab's soft under-belly and Aries will react with a defensive manoeuvre. And, as all Arians know, the best form of defence is attack.

Likewise, not just with family members but with his home base when he's an adult, Aries is proud of his home and very emotionally attached to and dependent on it. A secure home base is absolutely essential for him. Aries' generosity in his own home may surprise other people who have only seen the more aggressive side of him. If he trusts you enough to take you into his home, Aries will stuff you with food and drink until you almost burst. This is the Cancer influence on Aries again; feeding you is a way of nurturing and looking after you. Aries may well have a bossy, parental attitude to guests in his home, though!

Similarly, Aries parents are devoted to their children, but they can be rather aggressive about them and rather intolerably proud of them. They can also be over-demanding about their children, expecting them to achieve everything from the word go. They are not sensitive to more artistically inclined children. Aries children are deeply proud of their parents and can be quite exacting with them; they love them so much that any shortcomings are very hurtful to them.

FIFTH HOUSE (CREATIVITY)
Ruler Leo

Leo, the great emotional heart of Aries, rules its own fifth house, the house of creativity. So Aries is *always* doing something. He is driven to achieve anything and everything. Leo tells him that he is the rightful King and he must become this by virtue of what he does, so Aries is absolutely tireless. Aries is what he achieves in his life. And he must be admired for it; if others won't freely give him their devotion and flattery they damn well will have to so far as Aries is concerned. He will snow them under with his achievements and attain dominion over them. Aries rules because he *has* to. The urge to create is so deep in him, he can't know any rest. Aries *hates* relaxing. And, simply, Aries can create virtually anything; but he's best in some area of work where his aggression can be burned up, physically if possible, so other people don't get subjected to it.

Aries is passionate and regal in his love affairs. He is grand, generous, dignified, rather dramatic and just a little pompous. He is also a complete and utter chauvinist (this applies to female Arians too). He rules the roost so far as the partnership goes. He dominates the scene; both Aries and Leo are dominating signs. He may not always be faithful (Leo isn't entirely faithful), but he treats his lover magnificently and opulently. One thing he does lack, though, is a real sense of humour. His love affairs are deadly serious business for him; his pride is invested in them. If Aries is spurned in love his anger is implacable, and heaven help anyone stealing his lover away from him. Apart from the Scorpion, no-one makes a more determined enemy than an Arian whose pride is hurt. He will never forgive nor forget.

SIXTH HOUSE (WORK/SERVICE)
Ruler Virgo

Virgo's most obvious influence on Aries is the perfectionism of this sign. What Aries does is done well, with attention to detail and complete thoroughness. Aries is able to think through his work projects from start to finish and get things done. But often Aries himself is restless and not happy with what he has done. He is too perfectionist and he is very self-critical; again, this is Virgo's influence. Sometimes, indeed, Aries may abandon a work project which is going well simply because it doesn't quite measure up to his demanding standards. Anyone else would be happy with it (except for Virgos) but for Aries, 99% is simply not really good enough. If anything, Aries' pride exacerbates Virgo's faults; Virgo would settle for 99% (begrudgingly) but Aries cannot. But, nonetheless, Aries has great gifts as a craftsman and as a user of words (the Virgo influence again).

Where Virgo's influence is flatly countered by Aries is in the matter of service – the sixth sign and sixth house usually contain an element of service to others. Aries never served anyone, unless he could see his own ambition directly furthered by it. Aries is often at his best working alone, or directing others, since he really does not need anyone else to help him at work. He has the ability and initiative and financial planning may be the only area where he could use some help from time to time.

SEVENTH HOUSE (MARRIAGE/PARTNERSHIPS)
Ruler Libra

In marriage, Aries often seeks his opposite, and is attracted to a kind, gentler person than he is. His partner is often softer-spoken, more tactful, someone who is good at smoothing over quarrels which Arian aggression may have created. But there can certainly be strife in his marriage because his partner cannot handle all the aggression he has within him. Also, he's so proud of his partner that he is demanding of her and sometimes hurtful, with words or even physically. His partner is a projection of his own pride in himself, and just as he will expend great effort to make her look wonderful, he's terribly demanding of her. He wants everything to be just so. Libra's gentleness doesn't seem to be a quality affecting Aries himself in his marriage, rather his choice of mate. But sometimes the mix works; he *is* calmed and has his rough edges smoothed by his mate, and in turn his energy can stimulate 'lazy Libra' into doing things. It *can* work; it's just that it often doesn't.

Aries chooses similar types of people for business partnerships. Something in him (the Libra influence) does know that he can be over-pushy and too aggressive and it might be better if someone more diplomatic handled the public relations exercises. Aries is a brilliant company director but a disaster in personnel or public relations, and many Arians have the sense to realize this (those who don't will either learn fast or be chronically unemployable, or work alone as self-employed people).

EIGHTH HOUSE (NEEDS FROM OTHERS)
Ruler Scorpio

When Aries wants something, he gets it. What's more he knows he deserves it, almost by divine right. The intense force of Scorpio, coupled with Aries' energy and ambition, is the most potent combination imaginable. Aries expresses his needs with such force, power and directness that no-one can refuse him (not to his face, anyway). Aries may understand this and try to squeeze decisions from people when he's in face-to-face contact with them. This is an effective way for Aries to operate. He can impart a sense of urgency with Scorpio's power which makes someone listening to him feel that it really is imperative that Aries gets what he needs.

The compulsive, charismatic quality of Scorpio also acts in Aries' favour when his emotional needs are involved. It's not quite emotional blackmail, simply that Aries has the emotional force to get others to go along with him, and he's almost Svengali-like in this way.

The main problem for Aries is the Scorpio secretiveness with which he cloaks his needs. Others may be suspicious of him because (for example) he may protect what he sees as his vital interests with a web of intrigue or even deception. Aries may raise large sums of money but no-one is quite sure how, and no-one is entirely certain they want to trust him. Openness in important financial dealings is a crucial lesson for Aries.

NINTH HOUSE (FAR HORIZONS)
Ruler Sagittarius

Sagittarius brings some lightness to Aries' personality but it can fuel Aries' aggressiveness. Aries, when he lets his imagination wander and is lost in reverie, may have ideas for all sorts of things. His imagination is restless and ingenious. He is able to understand his work and activity in terms of higher goals and loftier ambitions. Aries, normally so occupied with his own ambition and pride, is capable of taking a more detached view of what he's doing in his more philosophical moods.

But Sagittarius has some pride about it too, and combined with Aries' aggression this can produce a fanatical person. Aries is convinced that his ideas about politics, religion and other social affairs are the right ones. Believing as he does that his instincts are humanitarian, and that he really *does* have the solutions, Aries becomes unbearable, a complete bigot. This only happens with some Aries people but very few of them are ever modest about their personal philosophy.

Sagittarius also gives Aries a strange wanderlust sometimes. Aries is a fiery, intense energy and Sagittarius can make this restless and changeable. Aries may hanker after travelling to broaden his mind, and to do this occasionally when the mood takes him is probably very good for him. Sometimes he can be unusually quiet when this mood takes him, receptive and eager to learn about different places and cultures.

TENTH HOUSE (CAREER)
Ruler Capricorn

Well, obviously Aries wants to rise to the top in his career; that almost goes without saying. And Capricorn does give him the practical gifts to do it. As we've seen, he can be meticulous in attention to detail at work, and Capricorn reinforces this. Something of Capricorn's patient nature can affect Aries; he can bide his time if he sees that an opening at the top is coming up at work. And he can work with great persistence on some work projects. Capricorn again gives him this ability.

Where conflict arises is in the area of authority. Aries does not always give others, in superior positions, the respect they deserve. They may not deserve it, of course, but it's as well not to say so too loudly in case they hear you. Old Jones down the corridor may well be past it but if he hears you say so, and he has the chairman's ear, you're in trouble. Aries doesn't understand this – or, rather, he doesn't *want* to understand this. Aries will *have* to learn some kind of diplomacy at work.

Also, while Aries can work with great persistence at what he's doing, it is hard for him to curb his ambitions. There are times to keep a low profile about such matters. Aries usually cannot do this, and this can be his downfall. Other people dislike him because of the nakedness of his ambition. Again, developing some elementary discretion is not a bad idea, although this is rather alien to Aries' nature. He cannot force his way to the top when the majority of people around him are against him.

Aries is not usually very popular with others at work; they resent his pushiness and he is not usually terribly considerate to people working for him. Self-employment, or careful choice of partner to handle other people at work, may be the answer for him.

ELEVENTH HOUSE (FRIENDSHIPS)
Ruler Aquarius

Aquarius' influence might be expected to make Aries a more sociable creature with many, varied and interesting friends. This is true – up to a point. Aries often does enjoy the company of unusual and rebellious kinds of people, and this may be bad for him – his own more rebellious and aggressive side may be kindled in such company. But the truth is that Aries' aggressiveness will often lead others to reject him; he is simply too much, too overwhelming for others to take. With this Aquarian influence, he wants to try ideas out on friends, put out feelers for his more unorthodox views; but, as usual, this is done with such forcefulness that others find him exhausting. Not really what you want for a lazy after-dinner conversation when the wine is settling nicely in the stomach (or the beer, or port, or brandy, depending on your tastes).

There is one solution to this. If Aries can burn off that aggressive side things may be easier; meeting friends through sporting activities can be one productive avenue of socializing for Aries. And one side of him often goes undeveloped or unnoticed; the Aquarian side makes him good at socializing with younger people, and in the role of (say) a leader of a venture group or a physical education teacher he can be very effective. Aries often likes younger people, possibly in part because Cancer's rulership of the fourth house makes him rather emotional about his own children and family.

TWELFTH HOUSE (THE UNCONSCIOUS)
Ruler Pisces

So, this is what is lacking in Aries' consciously developed personality. Pisces, the confused dreamer, whose love and affections are projected on to all humanity, is buried within Aries, and Piscean compassion is no part of him. Put brutally, Aries' problem is that he cannot love other people enough. His battering-ram aggression is, in the end, selfishness. Aries wants things for himself and his immediate family. He is devoid, really, of any altruistic or philanthropic instincts.

This is obviously a problem for the rest of us, but it's a problem for Aries too. Pisces will always make its influence felt, insidiously, little hints and glints rising from Aries' unconscious in daydreams and in his dream life and fantasies. Aries knows that somewhere within him is a better person, someone softer, gentler and less obsessed with *doing* things all the time. But Aries has no idea how to develop this. How can he? Pisces is confused enough anyway and this confusion is buried within the unconscious, so Aries has a doubled-up problem.

As with all twelfth house matters, the unconscious forces are most easily got to grips with in solitude and as the person gets older. When Aries has amassed his fortune, magnificent home and devoted family, and when making the next deal is beginning to become mechanical and the thrill is gone, he begins to turn within himself to reach out, tentatively, to this Piscean side. This is desperately difficult for Aries, because Pisces is so alien to his developed personality. Through psychoanalysis, or meditation, or reading imaginative fiction or religious works – anything with a Piscean streak – Aries can begin to let this Piscean influence enter his life. Unless the Piscean side is developed, Aries will die an unhappy and unfulfilled person. This is a very heavy way of putting things, but this really is the way things are; alone of all twelve signs, Aries has a hidden side which is the utter and complete opposite of his conscious mind *and* which is confused and nebulous into the bargain. Aries may, in the tiresome phrase, 'have it all' but without Pisces, he really has nothing at all.

☆ ☆ ☆

Aries is a powerful, aggressive, creative and dominating sign. Aries is the energy which gets many human achievements into practical shape and which gets things done. The rest of us may wince at Aries' forcefulness but we need his incredible energies. And, if his harshness is difficult to take at times, we might remember that with Pisces ruling his twelfth house he has the hardest problem in developing his personality of any of us. One cannot pity Aries – condescension to this sign is impossible – but understanding him should make us more tolerant of his more aggressive outbursts.

Taurus rising

THE BULL

Powerful and steadfast, the great bull symbolizes many of the strengths of Taurus. The person born with Taurus rising is indeed strong, staunch, earthy and very practical. Taurus is honest and fair; some people might feel, unfairly, that Taurus lacks the quick-mindedness to be a fluent deceiver but the truth is that dishonesty is completely alien to Taurus. And, although Taurus is rather down-to-earth, many Taurus people have a keenly developed sense of beauty. They enjoy beautiful things around them, and many have graceful ways of expressing themselves or are attracted to artistic careers. If one could sum up the virtues of Taurus in one word, it is *faithfulness*; they are honest partners in business, true friends and devoted partners.

But there is a flip side to this honest coinage. Taurus, being very practical, lacks imagination; a major shortcoming. Taurus often misses opportunities because, if he can't see an immediate pay-off, he doesn't think them worth pursuing. And Taurus can be habit-bound, and really rather dull as a person. Taurus is rather introverted anyway, and doesn't usually make an effort to be outgoing with others; even more extrovert Taurus people don't find it easy to express things dear to them and may tend to retreat into clichés and dull-dog conversation, just passing the time. Likewise, Taurus can have rather paranoid tendencies; once Taurus gets a wrong idea into his head about others (easily done if you don't have the imagination to think of other possibilities!), he sticks with it in the face of all conflicting evidence. Taurus can be very suspicious about other people, especially if his material wealth is involved. Taurus likes money and possessions; and he can be rather greedy and selfish about them.

So the general personality overlay of a person born with Taurus rising is bound up with steadfastness, practicality, and a lack of imagination. Let's see how these traits interact with more specific influences in the areas of life ruled by the houses.

SECOND HOUSE (MONEY)
Ruler Gemini

When it comes to making money, Taurus does not lack imagination. The sharp-witted influence of Gemini sees to that. Taurus is gifted at raising money through his ideas, through communicating them effectively to others and persuading them to go along with him. Moreover, his judgement is usually good because the general tendency of Taurus is careful, conservative. Taurus is very successful with money; the general and specific match up well. Gemini likes generating the ideas in the first place; the quicksilver mental influence of Gemini isn't bothered about getting things done. The general Taurus personality can be left to deal with that. A happy harmony here.

What's more, Taurus people will usually have their fingers in several financial pies; the versatility of Gemini ensures that. Nonetheless, no matter how many projects a Taurus gets involved with, they will always be carefully and practically checked. Taurus will not take risks if he can possibly help it. Nonetheless, some of them may be strikingly original applications of ideas to new practical problems; again, the practicality of Taurus and the versatility of Gemini.

You don't find many poor Taurus people!

THIRD HOUSE (COMMUNICATING)
Ruler Cancer

The distinction between *how* Taurus communicates, and *what* he communicates, is important. In speaking, or writing, Taurus has a natural sense of grace. It isn't embellished or affected; it's a natural thing for Taurus. Taurus speaks musically in many cases; his voice is very pleasing to hear. But he does not always find it easy to express himself. The general Taurus personality is, as we've seen, unimaginative in many cases and Cancer is too nervous and apprehensive an influence to help out. Taurus may find it very difficult to express his feelings, especially at home (the Cancer sphere of influence), and this can be a misery for him because Cancer is a deeply sensitive influence on his perceptions. Taurus can often be keenly aware of the moods and emotions of others; Cancer is responsive to such things and communicating is a two-way process.

A lot depends on whether Taurus feels he can deal with other people's emotional difficulties at such times. Often he feels that he can't – a lack of imagination again. What then happens is that the Cancer influence leads to an emotional retreat; the crab has a hard shell, and Taurus appears uncaring, even callous, when nothing of the sort is true. Taurus needs to stand back and force himself to think, when this happens, of how he can communicate effectively and *practically*: 'What can I suggest this person *do*?' – and not concern himself with feelings so much, but rather behaviour. This isn't easy; Cancer is concerned very much with underlying feelings, but it's the only way Taurus can escape this problem.

Obviously, Taurus people – just like anyone else – don't spend all their time communicating with others in settings of emotional tension! There are much more mundane things to life. But the Cancer influence is such that Taurus will always pick up on moods and feelings from others even in ordinary settings, at work or even on a train ride. He may feel it's a misfortune, but that's the way it has to be for him.

The other major problem Taurus can have in communicating with others is a lack of originality – he can be boring. Being so practical (so much of his originality is bound up with making money, not the most riveting topic of conversation at parties) he may not realize this for some time. And he may be rather moody and crotchety at times – the Cancer influence working directly on him. Taurus needs to make an effort to develop his interests and make them interesting for other people; learning about art, music or ballet are obvious possibilities for a Taurus with poor conversation skills, given his liking of such things.

Taurus has to make major efforts, in many cases, to communicate with others. But it's worth it; when others are drawn to him and realize his virtues, they'll put up with his lapses into moodiness and occasional emotional withdrawals.

FOURTH HOUSE (HOME)
Ruler Leo

So here is the emotional heart of Taurus: the 'Leo factor'. What is
closest to Taurus' heart is his love of home; and keep in mind that
the fourth house means more than just 'home' in the ordinary sense.
It means home, to be sure, and family life too, but above everything
it means a *base*, a secure place, where Taurus dwells and from
which he comes out to face the world and deal with others. Taurus
must have the security of a home base. Realizing this, we can see so
many other aspects of his personality in context. Taurus loves
money because of what it will do for him in providing him with a
secure base to live in (unlike, say, Capricorn rising which likes
money for itself). Taurus likes a large, spacious, beautiful home. He
is proud of his home, and he loves to show it off to friends. This is
the Leo influence coming through loud and clear; Leo's regal
qualities come through in Taurus as a host, inviting his friends to
admire his home. And Leo's generosity comes through too; nobody
ever went away hungry from a dinner at a Taurean's house. Nor did
they ever feel that their host didn't treat them with warmth and
affection!

Emotionally, Taurus has a deep attachment to family life. Taurus
parents are tremendously proud of their offspring – which can
produce two problems. They can be devoted to them even if they're
insufferable little beasts. This the Leo influence again – Leo does not
stand back and analyse anything. And, of course, Taurus rather
lacks the imagination to do that. Taurus parents should take rather
more detached looks at their children than they do – but advising
them to do that is fruitless. The other problem, more serious
perhaps (certainly for the Taurus parent) is that Taurus people can
be very possessive about their children (Taurus *is* generally possessive, and Leo is a rather possessive influence with things dear to the
person too). Allied to Taurus' lack of imagination – he finds it
difficult to understand how his children might want to do things he
doesn't know about or doesn't care for – there can be major
problems brewing here. Taurus parents have to learn to let their
growing children grow away from them in time, and that can be a
very hard lesson for them.

Taurus children, deeply attached to their parents as they usually
are, may likewise need some pushing out of the nest from wise

parents, and in the course of their growing up they need to have their imaginations stimulated by parents and teachers (this is obviously important for all children, but for Taurus children it's essential). Also, Taurus children are usually slow developers, and parents must understand that and have patience with them.

FIFTH HOUSE (CREATIVITY)
Ruler Virgo

Here again is harmony within the Taurus person. The cautious, analytical influence of Virgo means that, when creating things, the person with Taurus rising checks his ideas out carefully against practical possibilities. This is obviously very like the Taurus person's general personality. Virgo strives for perfection in things, and this is the only possible source of conflict; Taurus is practical enough to accept solutions to problems which are good enough to achieve what he wants. If 95% is good enough, why spend hours and hours thinking about how to get 99%? (Virgo would really like 100%, of course, but even Virgo isn't *that* perfectionist).

There is, though, one major problem here. The fifth house governs creativity, and also romance and affairs of the heart. Taurus people can be far too perfectionist about their loved ones in some cases (in others, their pride in them can lead to the opposite state of affairs). If the Virgo influence is strong, the Taurus person becomes almost impossible to live with. His partner will feel as if everything she does comes under the continual scrutiny of the Taurus person, and this makes life a misery. Likewise a Taurus woman will be a terrible nag if the Virgo influence predominates. A Taurus person who behaves like this is almost certainly going to have to learn the error of his ways the hard way, if he ever learns it at all. Once a Taurus person has a wrong idea in his head – and Virgo is absolutely *certain* that it's right and will justify the idea with every logical point at its disposal even if this is entirely missing the point – it won't be dislodged.

SIXTH HOUSE (WORK/SERVICE)
Ruler Libra

How happily the Libra influence fits with the general personality of Taurus! The amiable and friendly influence of Libra means that

Taurus people like working with others, and giving service if that's the kind of work they're drawn to. And Taurus' liking for money-making counteracts any adverse effects from the effects of 'lazy Libra'. Taurus people take pleasure working with others; it's something they want to do, and they can form many friendships with people they work with. Likewise, the charm of Libra ensures that workmates generally find Taurus people pleasant to work with – add that to the straightforward and honest general nature of those born with Taurus rising and things look pretty rosy. Taurus people are good bosses too; they treat their employees fairly and usually as equals.

Taurus people are, however, very concerned that they have pleasant environments to work in. Taurus likes beauty and dislikes dirtiness; and Libra won't tolerate anything unpleasant. So Taurus people make major efforts to brighten up workplaces and they wouldn't (and definitely shouldn't) work in unpleasant surroundings.

The sixth house also governs health affairs, and Taurus' major problem is clear enough – overeating. Libra is rather self-indulgent, and Taurus will take great pleasure in cooking – especially for dinner parties – another excuse for showing off his home and indulging his friends. And himself. Taurus may need to plan for cutting calorie intake – which he will hate!

SEVENTH HOUSE (MARRIAGE/PARTNERSHIPS)
Ruler Scorpio

The somewhat dark passions of Scorpio ensure that Taurus people are very intense in marriage and with their partners. And, of course, they are so deeply attached to home life anyway that light-heartedness in close partnerships may be very hard for them. A major problem Scorpio brings – and Taurus people are prone to this anyway – is suspiciousness. Taurus people are so proud of their partners, and so devoted to them, that they easily become over-possessive and regard any attempt by partners to develop their own lives away from the partnership with some concern. This is not easy for Taurus people to handle; Scorpio is not amenable to the powers of argument. Nonetheless, they have to come to terms with it. It may be easiest if the partner's individual efforts are clearly bringing material rewards of their own; then Taurus can see some return on things! But at least the partner of a person with Taurus rising knows that his, or her, partner is truly devoted to them.

In close partnerships of other kinds – notably close business partnerships, but also in close friendships – Taurus people tend to be attracted by status and power; this is the Scorpio influence. Taurus people like magnetic, powerful, charismatic people as close friends and associates. Now this is double-edged. When things go right and the partnership is harmonious, the Taurus person almost seems to draw power from his friend; but he can also be manipulated easily by a cunning person without realizing it. Neither the general Taurus personality, nor the specific Scorpio influence here, is too good at standing back and analysing what's going on coolly and calmly. Taurus can be suspicious, sure, but often about the wrong people! Taurus people sometimes do experience strong, magnetic attractions to others – not just sexually – and when this happens it may be as well to find out something about the people concerned.

EIGHTH HOUSE (NEEDS FROM OTHERS)
Ruler Sagittarius

The eighth house concerns *how* we project our needs to others, and also the responses we can expect from them, in general terms – and the benevolent influence of the lucky sign Sagittarius brings good fortune to Taurus people here. Taurus people do find it relatively easy to express ideas and projects to other people and to get favourable responses from them. Note that these are material needs, for the most part; emotional needs are another matter. The Sagittarian influence gives Taurus versatility at projecting his ideas to others, and the enthusiasm and optimism of Sagittarius is persuasive. When Taurus wants something and needs someone else to help him, it'll work out somehow. That's the way Sagittarius works.

The risk is of doing too much, spreading things too thin; making too many commitments to too many people, enlisting too many people to help out and collaborate on projects until Taurus loses track of what's going on. Fortunately, the generally practical nature of a person with Taurus rising tends to restrain this, but the Sagittarian over-enthusiasm needs keeping in check. The problem is that Taurus often needs to have several different things going on at once; he needs the challenge to stimulate his creativity and counter his tendencies to get stuck in a rut.

This is a difficult balancing act. The best solution for the Taurus person is to monitor carefully each project he has and who he has in mind for helping with it, working out his precise goals, what he's trying to do, how long it's going to take and what the alternatives are. This practical, ledger-keeping approach appeals to Taurus and it's the best way for him to go about things!

NINTH HOUSE (FAR HORIZONS)
Ruler Capricorn

Now we see why Taurus people so often lack imagination; ruling the house of imagination and dreams is Capricorn, the severely practical and hard-nosed sign of the goat. Taurus people distrust daydreaming and fantasies, and they are very conservative in their philosophy and religious beliefs. They tend also to be very material-istic about things; the influence of Capricorn ensures that, and that harmonizes with the general personality of Taurus rising. The Capricorn influence makes Taurus people very traditional in their outlook on life too.

But there is a positive side to this. The ninth house governs altruism, the desire to help others spurred on by humanitarian beliefs. The very practical influence of Capricorn here means that some Taurus people are able to put such motivations into effective action, perhaps in their work. Martin Luther King would be one of the most perfect examples of this in recent history. The noble quality of this ninth house drive in the person becomes almost a sense of duty under Capricorn's influence, indeed almost (without sounding too pretentious!) a sacred duty for the person. The twin influences of the Capricorn sign here and Taurus' general practi-cality can make the Taurus person one of the most powerful workers for the betterment of humanity among mankind.

TENTH HOUSE (CAREER)
Ruler Aquarius

Things get complicated here. The Aquarian influence is unor-thodox, impulsive and also inclined to like working in groups

(Aquarius, the eleventh sign, is associated with the eleventh house – of friendship). There can be several effects of these influences.

Aquarius likes unconventional, irregular work – odd hours, an unusual career, unconventional people to work with. This does *not* go well with what the general Taurus personality wants; Taurus wants security, practical work and good pay-offs. There can be a real conflict here, especially if Taurus gets stuck in a rut with his work. The impulsive quality of Aquarius can produce a major mistake for Taurus if it forces him to make a sudden break at work and move to something quite different. Taurus must resist this – and there are two ways of doing it.

The first is for Taurus to have several different involvements at once. This appeals to Taurus anyway, since Gemini ruling the second house of money pushes Taurus into diversifying. Aquarius gets bored easily and a change is as good as a rest.

The second solution is slightly trickier. Aquarius' gregarious tendencies tend to push Taurus into working with groups of people, often large groups, and that's fine for Taurus. There is one problem, though. Taurus can get attracted to working with charismatic, magnetic people and Aquarius loves this; but Taurus' judgement about such people is often poor. Taurus can be too impulsive and he needs to stand back and analyse his reactions to such people very carefully. Taurus needs a good friend to help him out here with sound advice, but unfortunately he may not be too wise in his choice of friends either – for reasons we'll shortly discover. But the Aquarian influence can be satisfied, and conflict avoided, if Taurus does make the right choice of unconventional dynamic people to work with.

ELEVENTH HOUSE (FRIENDSHIPS)
Ruler Pisces

Now we see why Taurus' choice of friends may not be too good; Pisces is hardly a clear-thinking influence for sound judgement! But the influence does make Taurus a valuable and appreciated friend.

One effect of the Pisces influence is that Taurus is very kindly and compassionate to his friends. Since he is also sensitive to their moods and emotions, this is a blessing for those friends but can be difficult for Taurus himself. Taurus can suffer too much from his ability to feel for his friends who are having troubled lives; Taurus will have to learn to stand back from that and be more dispassionate. His advice for them may not be too good on personal matters; his heart is in the right place but Pisces is not an influence bringing good judgement here.

Taurus also likes sharing his artistic inclinations, and his love of beautiful things, with his friends, and adding this to his natural sense of grace and balance in expressing himself makes him a charming friend. So, clearly, problems in friendships with Taurus don't usually affect his friends – they usually affect poor Taurus himself. Taurus will *have* to think out about his friends carefully, and by trial and error he will have to learn which ones are the ones he can rely on. Taurus can often be disillusioned when an unwise choice of friendship hurts him in some way, and that can turn into bitterness and suspicion. The only way out is for him to have a small group of trustworthy friends he can turn to at such times.

TWELFTH HOUSE (THE UNCONSCIOUS)
Ruler Aries

This house governs what is perhaps most difficult for the person to express about himself, and sometimes what may be an inner weakness. The rulership of Aries is hard for the Taurus person here, because Aries is a strong, aggressive, brute force when governing this twelfth house. On the one hand, Taurus often finds it very hard to express aggressiveness to others. And when he does, it may be rather violent, since the unconscious is not a balanced force. Taurus may fear expressing aggression; he may not understand that aggression, rather than destructiveness, is a perfectly healthy thing. Taurus may keep his aggression pent up and, if he is goaded by others, simply explode into violence. Taurus can have a powerful temper, slow to anger but incandescent with rage when he's finally pushed too far. A charging bull is a pretty fearsome thing. Because of the very physical nature of Aries and the general earthiness of Taurus, strenuous physical activity may be one way of dealing with this aggression. Channelling it into work is another way for the Taurus person to deal with it.

Also, Taurus may have problems with sex because of the hidden, obscured effect of the physical Aries influence. Taurus has a fairly healthy sexual appetite, but may have hidden complexes or frustrations, especially if these relate to the way in which he (or she) shows aggression in sexual behaviour. As with any twelfth house problems, these difficulties can be lessened when the person feels himself to be somewhere safe, in a reassuring environment. Which means with someone he trusts completely; but Taurus is so readily roused to suspiciousness about his partner that this may not be so easy for him. Trusting others – and trusting others wisely – is the most difficult life problem the Taurus person will have; it's his life task.

So, this is Taurus: not an easy sign to be born under, but a strong and honest one, and one easily loved by others. There is, truly, little malice or evil in Taurus, and the weaknesses of greed and suspicion arise most often from an inner insecurity, a craving for safety, both materially and emotionally. These are not such terrible failings; the rest of us should be pleased with the Bull's place in the scheme of things.

Gemini rising
THE TWINS

Brilliant and mercurial, the symbol for Gemini is the first in the Zodiac to show human beings. How right this is, when Gemini is all about the power of reason and thought, those uniquely human abilities! Gemini is sharp-witted, fast-thinking, and can argue the hind legs off a donkey. And yet Gemini is not an intellectual, really; and again the symbol of the twins shows us why. Twins are *two*; and Gemini's mind is too quicksilver, too rapidly moving from one thing to another to concern itself with anything profound. Not that this worries Gemini. Once I was describing Gemini to an acquaintance as a rather superficial sign, and a Gemini overhearing the conversation (the kind of thing Gemini loves doing; Gemini wants to hear and know every bit of trivial communication and gossip possible) burst in and said brightly, 'that's right!'. Gemini would rather do crossword puzzles than read textbooks of philosophy. But what a mind nonetheless – no-one thinks faster than Gemini. Gemini often dominates circles of friends and acquaintances by sheer speed of thought – and Gemini is so gregarious that those circles are usually very large.

In addition to superficiality, perhaps Gemini's major failing is his inability to handle slower-thinking or emotionally sensitive, people. Gemini has no patience with them, and can often mock them cruelly, using all the dazzling talent of his clever talk to do it. It's not that Gemini wants to hurt; this is almost a game for Gemini, and he simply doesn't understand emotional depths or over-sensitivity. In this way he's very like Sagittarius, the ninth sign, opposite Gemini in the wheel of the Zodiac, with whom he has much in common. Gemini can be a curiously passionless person, motivated simply by the love of his own brilliance in thinking and speech – yet he's not as egotistical as that suggests. Complicated – but Gemini is a dual sign, changeable and restless, forever on the move one way or another. How can one describe him when it's almost impossible even to keep up with him? We can but try.

The general personality overlay of the person born with Gemini rising is bound up, then, with mental speed and with thinking as the dominant way of dealing with everything.

SECOND HOUSE (MONEY)
Ruler Cancer

We start with what seems to be a paradox; how suitable for Gemini. The emotionally responsive, moody quality of Cancer affects how Gemini earns and uses his money. How can this fit with Gemini's predominantly mental approach to life when something so crucial is involved? Rather well, in many cases.

What the Cancer influence brings is this: although Gemini is often insensitive to the emotions of others as individuals, he often has an uncanny sensitivity to people's needs as these relate to how to earn money. Gemini knows what the market wants, to use ad men's parlance – and this does fit with the general Gemini personality perfectly. The Cancer influence tells Gemini instinctively what people want and Gemini knows exactly how to give it to them and how to sell it to them. What's more, the emotionally fluctuating quality of Cancer makes Gemini responsive to shifting demands, changes in fashion; Gemini is always one step ahead of the latest market changes. And how Gemini loves putting his mind to such things! So what seems to be a paradox isn't; things fit neatly.

Also, Gemini tends to link what emotional needs he does have to financial affairs, given this Cancer influence on the second house. Although Gemini is impulsive and restless, he's a planner, and he may often have a nest-egg tucked away, carefully thought-out insurance policies for himself and his home, and so on. This gives Gemini a feeling of emotional security and makes him feel freer to devote his time to using his intellect.

The only possible problem for Gemini here is over-restlessness with his money; impulse spending, carelessness with investing in things which 'feel' right (the unthinking Cancer influence) and the like. But Gemini is usually too careful a thinker to fall into *that* trap.

THIRD HOUSE (COMMUNICATING)
Ruler Leo

And now we see just why Gemini is the thinker. The Leo factor in him pushes him this way; his deepest desire is to communicate with others, to influence them by the power of his intellect, to use reason as his tool for dealing with the world. Gemini (like Sagittarius) is a 'perfect' sign in this way; Leo rules the third house, the affairs naturally associated anyway with Gemini (as the third sign). And this explains Gemini's gregariousness; if communicating is his deepest desire, he wants as many people to communicate with as possible.

Geminis invest all their power into expressing their intellect and creativity to others, through any mode of communicating; writing, speaking, acting, politics, lecturing, anything. And it's the power of their own ideas they want to express; it's their originality and creativity. How could it be otherwise with Leo ruling this house? Gemini may be an advertising man, an actor, journalist, writer, computer software designer, a marriage guidance counsellor – anything where expressing his ideas to others is the keynote of what he's doing. And there is no possible conflict in the affairs of the third house; perfect harmony between the general personality and the deepest desire of Gemini. Which explains why Gemini, while being restless, is not a nervous sign; this very basic harmony within him precludes that!

FOURTH HOUSE (HOME)
Ruler Virgo

More harmony here. The analytical quality of Virgo affects Gemini's home life, and that's in keeping with Gemini's preference for thinking over feeling. There are several effects of this.

Gemini often works from home or does much of his work at home; Virgo is associated with work and service and it's a natural development for Gemini. Certainly Gemini does not leave his work at the office! Work and home life are not to be separated for him. And work can become a way in which Gemini provides for his home and family; of course, that's true of everyone, but with Gemini the two are very intimately linked. But there can be problems; Gemini thinks that his family should approve of his bringing work home with him since it's providing for them and this is logically sensible. Unfortunately his family may not be moved by cold logic pure and simple. Gemini may need forcibly separating from his ledgers, writings and papers.

The Virgo influence makes Gemini very fastidious about home life. Gemini can be extremely untidy but loathes dirt around his home. He's likely to have a very modern, very efficiently designed home, which (underneath all the debris) is immaculately clean. It's also likely to have radios, televisions, home computers, cameras, videos and all the other means of communication Gemini can afford to cram into it.

Gemini as a parent and spouse can have problems, though. As a parent, his analysis of what's right for his children is very sound. Children of Geminis will not lack for a stimulating education and Gemini knows how to foster and develop a child's sense of wonder and turn it into a desire to learn. But Gemini may not express affection easily and his children may feel unloved. This is not easy for Gemini to deal with; he will have to make real efforts here. Likewise, Gemini children are bright, energetic little creatures but often curiously detached from their parents. However, their parents can command their genuine affection if they provide them with many ways of stimulating their minds. Just provide plenty of books, pictures and the rest and leave it to the Gemini child. He needs little direction in his education!

FIFTH HOUSE (CREATIVITY)
Ruler Libra

Gemini's gregariousness is reinforced by Libra's influence. Libra likes working with others; it's friendly and charming influence strengthens Gemini's drive to communicate with others and also provides him with the graces to do it effectively, working well with other people to express his ideas and creativity. Also, the Libra influence – with its natural sense of balance and refinements – tends to pick the right people for working with. Geminis are attracted to graceful, pleasant people to work with and express their ideas with (but they'll certainly tend to dominate them; Gemini tends to do this anyway and, as we'll see, the eleventh house shows this too).

Libra also brings some artistic abilities to Gemini's creativity – which is why he can function not just as (say) a journalist or writer but as something more directly creative such as an actor (and how well *that* fits with Gemini's versatility and love of changes).

In romance, Libra is a delightful influence on Gemini. Gemini's coolness in emotional matters is compensated for by the grace of Libra; he is attentive, charming, immaculately mannered and showers the object of his affections with beautiful things. Gemini is also very much concerned with beauty in whoever he is attracted to; the Libra influence demands that. Gemini doesn't want a grand passion but he does want someone who is at least pretty and reasonably intelligent into the bargain! A hard person to satisfy – and Gemini is not even given to the fidelity which might make him really worth it. Geminis often have casual affairs, mistresses and lovers; the dual nature of the twins again. In fact, it has to be said that while Geminis make charming lovers, they really don't make very satisfactory husbands or wives. They really are better off bright-eyed and bushy-tailed looking for the next whirlwind romantic fling. However, they'll probably plead with every smooth phrase at their command (of which they have many) that this really *is* the love of their life, for at least a few weeks!

SIXTH HOUSE (WORK/SERVICE)
Ruler Scorpio

Gemini *must* work; the powerful drive of Scorpio compels him to. And Scorpio ruling this house gives Gemini real power when he communicates with others in his chosen field of work; he can persuade people to comply with his ideas not just because of his fast mind and remorseless logic – the general Gemini personality – but because he is a rather good manipulator too. Sometimes this is conscious; Gemini can be a calculating person. But just as often it is an unconscious process; the magnetism of Scorpio almost seduces those who listen to Gemini. The combination of charisma and reason is very powerful.

There's also an intensity from this Scorpio influence which gives Gemini a cutting edge in his work; the usually cool and rather logical Gemini mind has to apply itself, has to produce things; the communications must have effects which Gemini can see. Scorpio demands results. And this is personally vital to Gemini; he measures his own value in terms of how effective he is at communicating his ideas and turning them into practically useable products and applications. This, of course, harmonizes with the Leo factor in Gemini's personality.

The sixth house also governs affairs of health, and the Scorpio rulership indicates a need for Geminis to avoid being absolute workaholics on the one hand (a problem which may affect their home lives as well as their health) and suffering health problems from frustrations at work, usually nervous complaints or psycho-somatic problems. Geminis should force themselves to take regular holidays — and have plenty to do when they get back — to keep a balance here.

SEVENTH HOUSE (MARRIAGE PARTNERSHIPS)
Ruler Sagittarius

The qualities of Sagittarius affect how Geminis act towards their close friends and lovers and what qualities they seek in them. Sagittarius is every bit as changeable and restless as Gemini, so the specific influence of Sagittarius just reinforces Gemini's liking for many and varied friends. Also, Gemini looks for intellectual, intelligent friends even in close friendships, and with lovers he demands these qualities too (as well as beauty, as we saw from his fifth house rulership by Libra). In turn, Gemini wants to exchange ideas above everything with close friends; another spur to the great communicator's drive to express himself and convey his ideas.

Something of the luckiness of Sagittarius applies to Gemini's choice of close friends; they tend to be supportive to him and he has the knack of choosing the right people to befriend, people who are honest and generous to him. Gemini also likes a good sense of humour in close friends, and while he likes intellectuals anything too serious and lacking in the ability to laugh at life is what he most wishes to avoid.

Likewise, Geminis tend to be lucky in affairs and marriage; their partners often are pretty or handsome, witty and intelligent. And they may even have the good luck (if that's what it is, and a Gemini would see it that way) to turn a blind eye to their occasional romantic flings elsewhere.

The one problem for Gemini is of having too many friends, being over-expansive, spreading himself too thin, and the possibility of financial errors made with respect to friends. But Gemini is usually too financially careful to make such mistakes, and is clear-thinking enough to evaluate his friends coolly and calmly. And there's always the luck Sagittarius brings in such matters!

EIGHTH HOUSE (NEEDS FROM OTHERS)
Ruler Capricorn

Here, for once, all is not sweetness and light. The heavy, dutiful influence of Capricorn weighs heavily on Gemini. The Gemini mind, above all, wants to be unfettered and free to express itself how and whither it pleases, and 'duty' is a very alien concept to a Gemini. But Capricorn's influence means that where Gemini must express directly his needs to others, there is a weight on him. This is less true psychologically and emotionally (since Gemini does not, frankly, have major deep psychological needs other than that for a good audience) so much as materially. Gemini hates admitting he needs to borrow money, for example, and if he does have to arrange a loan or something similar he will procrastinate and probably pretend he needs less than he does and twist himself in knots justifying himself up to the hilt. Gemini simply *hates* this.

On the other hand, the Capricorn influence gives Gemini a feeling inside himself that in partnerships and business affairs he needs to earn his fair share. Capricorn won't stoop to cheating or deceptions and insists on fair dealing. Maybe this specific influence of Capricorn is as well for everyone else, since of all the signs Gemini has the greatest ability for scheming and machination. But Capricorn won't let him do it, and if he does he'll suffer miseries of guilt for years. So Geminis tend to be honest and straightforward in business dealings with others; they just often don't like admitting that they need assistance when they do.

NINTH HOUSE (FAR HORIZONS)
Ruler Aquarius

Again, we can see here why Gemini has the reputation for being not just an able communicator but a versatile and original one. The unconventional, free-thinking and sometimes rebellious Aquarian influence rules the house of daydreaming and imagination. In his fantasies and idle thinking moments, Gemini can come up with truly original ideas, which his inventive mind can then pick up, analyse, and put into concrete form. Geminis often get sudden inspiration, 'Eureka!' moments when the germ of some new idea comes to them. This is a happy combination, the insight of Aquarius and the logic of Gemini. It gives Gemini a quality of inventiveness, insightfulness; something with substance for him to communicate, and how well that fits with the other drives within him.

Since religion and philosophy are affairs of the ninth house, Geminis often have unconventional ideas on these matters which they are only too happy to exhaust others with at some length. The sudden-inspiration quality of Aquarius can also prompt Geminis to distant travel (ninth house) in pursuit of their ideas or work associated with it.

The two major problems here are linked; different sides of the same coin. On the one hand, Geminis who are taken with avant-garde thinking about religion, philosophy or life in general and views thereupon can be rather tediously fanatical about it (a typical Aquarian effect). On the other hand, they can be restless and impulsive about things so that it's just a question of which guru they're following this week. However, Geminis afflicted in these ways can usually readily accept criticism from friends about it. It's almost impossible to offend Gemini with such criticism; his love of exchanging ideas is too great for that. But every Gemini needs a friend who will tell him when he is talking nonsense, and usually they're lucky enough to have several.

TENTH HOUSE (CAREER)
Ruler Pisces

Problems. Gemini is a great communicator, and has original and versatile ideas to get across, but how? What career to adopt? Pisces must be the worst influence imaginable on the house of career. There is an unrealistic, unworldly approach to such matters by many Geminis, reflecting this Pisces influence. They may be vision-aries with great ideas, or they may desperately want to do some-thing useful to other people without knowing quite what or just how to do it. The problem of this Pisces influence pinpoints Gemini's major difficulty in life: the need to be practical idealists in work. Work is of central importance to Gemini (the influences of Leo ruling the third house and Scorpio ruling the sixth) and yet he often doesn't know just what to do. Geminis, indeed, are often difficult to pin down about their professional lives, and there may be peculiar work conditions or conditions attached to their jobs. They may be elusive in talking about exactly what it is that they actually do, reflecting ambiguities in their work lives or a strange reluctance to explain their motivations for work. The confusions of Pisces bring such peculiarities to Gemini's personality, and like Gemini Pisces is also mutable, changeable and restless, adding further difficulties.

Young Geminis badly need career guidance, because they often don't know or understand what they actually want to do or, if they do, how to go about doing it. Wise parents of Geminis will take this problem on reasonably early. The prime need for Gemini is practicality: 'What do I want to do, exactly? And in what careers can I satisfy this desire, that motivation, this ambition?' Gemini needs to read the fine print in work contracts, to force himself to analyse carefully what he's doing and what can be expected from it. This can appeal to the Gemini mind, that the strange and irrational, almost contrary, influence of Pisces can undermine this unless closely controlled. Which Gemini *must* do.

Likewise Gemini may make mistakes with workmates at times, being too unrealistic about them, expecting too much or overlooking dishonesties by others. Usually Gemini is naturally lucky with such contacts, but it's a problem he needs to watch. For Gemini's workmates, things are happier – the Piscean influence makes Gemini naturally responsive and sympathetic to the feelings of those he works with, at least on first impulse, and the Capricorn influence on Gemini's eighth house makes him earn his way in work groups. A happy combination – but that razor-sharp mind can still dominate anyone around.

In many ways, the actor would be the perfect career choice for Gemini, but his problem is: 'What role shall I play, and for how long?' Every Gemini has to find his own answers to these questions.

ELEVENTH HOUSE (FRIENDSHIPS)
Ruler Aries

Not only are Geminis gregarious, they're *aggressively* sociable. Since the eleventh house concerns distant acquaintances and ordinary friendships rather than intimate partnerships, the energy of Aries means that Gemini has many circles of acquaintances and socializes a great deal at relatively superficial levels. This Aries energy fits well with Gemini's role as a communicator; Gemini puts much effort into collecting friends and is constantly looking for new and more varied circles of friends.

The Aries influence also makes Gemini very active; he won't be finding his friends in quiet or secluded places but at noisy parties, in tennis or golf clubs or somewhere where an active sport is going on, at debating societies, anywhere where there's a lot of *activity*. The Aries influence demands activity and stimulation from friendships, and Gemini is easily bored anyway. Some edge of competition in these friendships is demanded by the aggressive Aries influence, so debating or sports clubs where Gemini can burn up this aggressive energy are good places for him to encounter new friends.

However, Gemini can easily neglect or forget old friends in his constant search for new, exciting friends elsewhere. Aries is a 'pushy' influence not much given to sentiment about old friends, and Gemini isn't a sentimental sign in any case. Gemini may not easily understand how friends don't like being cast aside for new ones at the drop of a hat. Gemini has to learn to be more sensitive to this problem, and keeping a social diary and checking it occasionally to see if certain friends have been neglected is a sound move.

TWELFTH HOUSE (THE UNCONSCIOUS)
Ruler Taurus

One effect of the Taurus influence on the unconscious is that Gemini often secretly craves what is dearest to Taurus; money, beautiful things and security. The first two aren't so great a problem – Gemini likes beauty in his partners and indeed demands it, and is often a careful planner with money, as we've seen. But the security angle is more difficult, for Gemini is generally restless and likes change, which Taurus doesn't want to put up with at all. Gemini is often confused about career plans, and Taurus most certainly wants security there, which can add to Gemini's anxiety. Still, at least with money, Gemini's ability to plan things carefully can go a long way to assuaging Taurus' fears. But a weakness in Gemini can be an unconscious selfishness, a greediness, which will afflict him if he doesn't have sufficient security.

On the other hand, the Taurus influence gives a persistence to Gemini's drives and needs which might otherwise be lacking. In pursuit of what he wants, Gemini can be quite determined. Without the Taurus influence, a thwarted Gemini might be tempted to avoid problems and move to something else, forever evading difficulties, but the Taurus influence – one of some stubbornness – makes Gemini use his mind to find new solutions to problems instead.

Someone once suggested that, if there had been an animal symbol for Gemini in the Zodiac, it would surely be the monkey, chattering away. There's some truth in that, but it does Gemini poor service. The force and speed of his mind is too well developed for any animal to represent as a symbol! Teacher, communicator, persuader and developer of ideas, people born under the other eleven signs would be much worse off without Gemini to stimulate, challenge, and usually outwit them!

Cancer rising
THE CRAB

In astrology, Cancer is ruled by the Moon, and the emotional waxing and waning and the moodiness of Cancer is well known. Cancer is a protective, emotional, often fearful sign, introverted and with great emotional depths. But there's another side, which the symbol of the crab shows us. Crabs have large and powerful claws, and a frightened or threatened Cancer person has powerful retaliatory abilities. Also, the crab has a hard shell into which it retreats if threatened, and likewise Cancer people often retreat and withdraw from others if anxious or hurt. But what is inside the shell is soft and easily hurt. Cancer is not an easy sign to be born under, because there's a basic insecurity within Cancer people which often makes them feel threatened when they're not.

Cancer is well known as the sign of the home and the mother, and Cancer people – men as well as women – are protective, maternal, very loving people. But they are moody and can be very possessive about others because of their inner insecurity. Cancer is not a thinking, analytical sign because it's all about *feelings* with Cancer people; feelings, their own and others, concern them most of the time, and they will often say 'I feel that . . .' rather than 'I think that . . .'. The general personality overlay for the Cancer person is that of *emotional responding* to everything and everyone around them; their reactions come from the heart, not from the head. But their emotional depths contain many surprises which are not obvious to insensitive observers of Cancer people. Let's take a closer look at the Cancer personality.

SECOND HOUSE (MONEY)
Ruler Leo

Now *this* is a surprise for a start. The Leo factor in the Cancer person, the thing most important to them, is money. How can this possibly fit with the well-known emotional quality of Cancer? Materialism hardly seems to fit.

But it does – because Cancer craves money and material wealth as *security*; most particularly, security for the *home*. Cancer craves a safe base, a guaranteed rock-solid domestic base, a place where his family can be safe. Craving for this security, guaranteed by earnings, is bound up with Cancer's sense of self-esteem and his feelings of his own worth (the Leo influence), and Cancer measures his own self-worth in material terms at times. This is reinforced by Aries ruling the tenth house, but more of that later. Cancer invests great energy into earning money, and feels personally threatened if he is not financially secure. Impoverished Cancer people can experience very great depressions, the natural Cancer reaction to such adverse circumstances.

Cancer has to learn that his worth as a person is *not* measured in terms of how much money he has – not by other people, anyway. His friends and partners need to understand that Cancer is not greedy; he doesn't want money for itself, but for the sense of security it brings him, and he may need much reassurance from others that he isn't worthless just because he isn't wealthy. Fortunately, Cancer's emotionally responsive quality means that this feedback from friends can be effective – but only in the short term. Cancer is too emotionally changeable for that, and his underlying anxieties will return.

The Leo influence also means that Cancer people often earn money by being in some position of authority (the regal quality of Leo) and this can be anything from a company executive to secretary of some club, a job bringing in an amount small in relative terms but precious to Cancer's need for security. Since Cancers are ambitious in their careers, they tend to find their ways into such positions surprisingly easily.

THIRD HOUSE (COMMUNICATING)
Ruler Virgo

Cancer tends to introversion; his own emotions and his family life and home are what preoccupy him. Cancer is not particularly outgoing, and Virgo ruling the third house doesn't make socializing and communicating with others easier. Cancers are careful about how they express themselves (except when emotionally aroused); the precise and analysing quality of Virgo makes this so. The crab's claws come into the picture too; Virgo is a critical and demanding influence and Cancer people can be quite withering and sarcastic in speech. They can, in particular, be quite critical about home and family life, which creates tension in them, given their deep need for emotional security and harmony at home and with their loved ones.

However, there's a very positive side to this. Cancers are very precise and correct in their expressions, speaking and writing, and with almost any kind of clerical activity they are fine workers. Cancers keep precise ledgers, minutes of meetings, accounts and the like, and send precise and brief memos to others. They have the ability to convey to others exactly what needs communicating, precisely and with no wasted words. These talents have obvious value to them at work. Even at home they will have shopping lists of everything they need and nothing superfluous!

And Cancer people *can* communicate their needs and ideas very effectively to others, given this Virgo influence. Although their reactions are usually based on emotion, Virgo gives them the possibility of more cool-headed, logically thought-out dealings with other people so long as nothing of central importance to their security (as they see it) is involved.

Cancer people often underestimate their own abilities to persuade others in conversation and to express their ideas clearly; part of the general insecurity which plagues this sign. But these capacities are most definitely there!

FOURTH HOUSE (HOME)
Ruler Libra

Cancer people cannot abide disharmony in the home. Emotional conflicts in families almost paralyse Cancer with unhappiness; they often retreat within themselves and nurse their hurts, trying to avoid the conflicts. Alas, this doesn't work. Cancer doesn't forget or forgive easily, and a real or imagined painful episode will be gone over in Cancer's mind again and again and will eventually produce an emotional outburst some time after the event, which can be mystifying and infuriating for other people. . . And, since Libra is not an influence bringing hard work or activity to Cancer, Cancer may oddly enough not truly work at creating domestic harmony as much as he might. In particular, he may avoid domestic problems rather than confront them. Cancer people will have to learn to do this, hard as the lesson will be.

But Cancer himself rarely causes such domestic problems, at least not through any negative qualities. The balancing influence of Libra means that Cancer people are very fair in domestic dealings, treating family members equally and justly. They also go to great lengths to make life for their families happy by creating a beautiful home (Libra's love of beauty) – after all, they're not happy themselves unless their home is a lovely place.

Cancer's love of home is so great that a young adult Cancer person may often retreat to his parents' home in times of stress – part of a general problem with Cancer's home life. Cancer parents can be very possessive about their children, and when they leave home the Cancer parent often feels rejected. Cancer may make great efforts to keep in touch with his children, even if this is intrusive or annoying to them. This can bring about a real rejection by the irritated offspring, which will hurt Cancer very badly and possibly produce a cruel and rejecting reaction in turn (the crab has claws). It may all be smoothed over in the end – Libra's love of harmony may make it so – but Cancer parents have to understand their over-possessiveness here. Cancer parents are also often fearful about their children's welfare – fine for a child of seven but not for a seventeen-year-old. They may try to avoid their children's potential problems for them, a classic parental error. Learning to let go is a major life lesson for the Cancer parent. And something similar is true of Cancer children – just like Taurus children, they need to be pushed gently out of the parental nest, but it must be done slowly, and the whole business is more emotionally fraught than for Taurus. The best solution is to do things gently, step by step; it's catastrophic for a Cancer suddenly to break loose. Another important thing for a parent or child of a Cancer person to remember is that the feeling of security needs to be in Cancer's mind; if Cancer has an address, a telephone number, some way of getting in touch, he will feel much better. So much of this is in Cancer's mind rather than in the way things really are, that such emotional reassurance is badly needed by them – and not much of a price to pay for the love and affection they shower on their families.

FIFTH HOUSE (CREATIVITY)
Ruler Scorpio

Since Cancer is an emotional sign, and Scorpio legendarily the sign of deep and passionate emotion, the affairs of the fifth house revolve around the romantic affairs governed by it. Cancer has considerable problems with his love life. First, he's often attracted to the wrong person. The Scorpio influence wants someone magnetic, charismatic, a grand passion, which fits well with Cancer's generally emotional nature. But Scorpio has a yearning for the unusual, even the dangerous; a femme fatale rather than a partner for life (even though this is exactly what Cancer does want). A typical error made by Cancer people is to feel, with every last ounce of emotion in them (which is a lot), that through the power of their love they can transform the loved one; this is the Scorpio influence, since Scorpio has much to do with major upheavals and transformations in emotional life. It usually doesn't work this way; Cancer often selects precisely the wrong person, and the notion is a hopelessly romantic one anyway (but wouldn't a Cancer person despise that phrase!).

Cancer people are intensely passionate emotionally and sexually; they are also very sensuous, indulging their senses in romance through good food, wine, candlelit dinners for two, red roses, fine clothes, exotic scents and perfumes and just about anything else they can think of (though for a Cancer, it would be 'feel for' rather than 'think of'). In such ways, they express themselves creatively – and this is often bound up with their home lives, since their home is where their partner is (if Cancer has what he desires) and home life is so crucial to them anyway. The Scorpio influence reinforces Cancer's efforts in creating a beautiful home, and the energies of Scorpio usually overcome Libra's laziness.

But Cancer's passions are so deep that, coupled with the insecurity of this sign, Cancer easily becomes jealous of partners. The Scorpio influence makes things even worse here. Cancer people can easily feel as if they live only for the ones they love, and their

emotions are so powerful that they expect this complete commitment from others too. If it isn't forthcoming – and it would be hard
to match a Cancer person for absolute devotion – Cancer may
become jealous, critical and embittered.

It's clear that there may be major problems for Cancer people
here. What they badly need is a close friend to turn to for help,
sympathy and general advice at such times. How this works is an
affair of the eleventh house, but it's an essential for Cancer. Married
confidantes of the same sex make especially good friends for Cancer
in the matter of helping them with their own domestic troubles.

SIXTH HOUSE (WORK/SERVICE)
Ruler Sagittarius

The fortunate influence of Sagittarius tends to counter Cancer's
somewhat insecure personality in work; Cancers are ambitious
and, while they may sometimes feel anxieties and insecurity about
work, usually something inside them is hopeful, optimistic and even
enthusiastic about it. The Sagittarian influence gives Cancer a
feeling that everything may, after all, turn out well at work – just as
well, since their need for financial security is rather great! There's
also a generosity with others at work under this influence; just as
Cancer treats family members fairly (Libra ruling the fourth) he
treats co-workers well and this is appreciated. Cancer is especially
helpful to young people at work; Sagittarian generosity and
Cancer's maternal nature working together.

Sagittarius is sometimes inclined to lofty ideals and, with Cancer's drive to give emotionally to others, Cancer people can be
devoted servants of others' wishes and needs at work – sometimes
(Aries ruling the tenth isn't so happy about that). But Cancer people
do need to find their own sphere of work and they can get bored
easily (Sagittarius again), becoming moody and irritable when that
happens. Cancer does, though, have the Sagittarian energy to
diversify at work, but this is often only after some time and no little
grumbling about it.

Cancers can have health problems (the other major sixth house
concern) from over-indulgence. Good eating may be part and parcel
of Cancer's nurturing personality at home, and Sagittarius is hardly
a moderating influence. Overeating of rich foods can be an especial
problem. Indeed, when depressed, Cancer people can overeat badly,

since taking in nourishment in this way can seem like a substitute for love and affection in some way. Cancer people must make a major effort not to do this when unhappy or depressed.

SEVENTH HOUSE (MARRIAGE/PARTNERSHIPS)
Ruler Capricorn

Capricorn is something of a sobering influence on Cancer when marriage and intimate partnerships are involved. Cancer is intensely emotionally responsive, and Scorpio's rulership of the fifth house adds to that, but Capricorn wants to be practical about things. Usually, what this means is that Cancer people are practical about marriages when they're married but not before. Although Capricorn should make a Cancer person careful about marriage, it often doesn't work that way. Since the influence of Capricorn often means late achievement of things, what may happen with many Cancer people is that a first unsuited marriage is followed in middle age by a much happier one, or (for luckier Cancer people) that they don't marry in the first place until Mr or Ms Right comes along after the first flush of youth. Capricorn's influence also goes well with Libra's motivation towards fairness at home; Capricorn invents ways of making domestic fairness work, even in matters as mundane as rotas for who does the cooking at Sunday lunchtimes! And yet Capricorn can exacerbate Cancer's insecurity, for Capricorn demands security too, so there is a double drive for security in marriage which can make Cancer's jealousy all the worse.

In partnerships in business life, Cancer people are very careful. They select partners prudently and after a lot of consideration, checking their financial and practical worth rather carefully. Cancer may often want to stay behind the scenes in such dealings; both Cancer and Capricorn are introvert signs and Cancer will be happier doing the work while someone else does the public relations bit. And this is a good way of going about things, for Capricorn's constructive energies suit Cancer perfectly in this role.

EIGHTH HOUSE (NEEDS FROM OTHERS)
Ruler Aquarius

The rulership by Aquarius of this house, governing as it does how the Cancer person expresses his needs to others and their responses, brings some surprises. Aquarius is outgoing and inventive, and while Cancer is generally rather withdrawn from others, when something Cancer needs (or feels he needs, which is the same thing for a Cancer person) is involved he can be ingenious and original in expressing that need to others. Cancer may be very adept at communicating financial or emotional needs to others – and precise about it at the same time (Virgo ruling the third house).

The unconventional Aquarius influence colours the Cancer personality in another way. Cancer people are interested in spirituality, religion, psychic matters – 'the power of positive thinking'. They are intrigued by such things, in many cases, and how they fit in with human affairs, and they enjoy talking about them with people they feel emotionally secure with. Cancer people may often have experiences of telepathy or precognition – almost always involving other people and not just objective events of some kind – and they may enjoy discussing them and their implications with close friends. They are also sensitive to such things in other people and make sympathetic listeners to those who have had psychic experiences and who have been misunderstood by others.

However, Aquarius is also rebellious and impulsive, even though it is a 'thinking' sign, and if there's a problem pinpointed here it is this: Cancer people may often leave expressing their needs to others until the last minute, or do so impulsively and in some unorthodox or unacceptable way. This is most likely to happen when the Cancer person is feeling moody or irritable. Cancer people should be careful about expressing needs in negative moods or too impulsively, even if the solution is the old one of counting to ten mentally while biting one's tongue.

NINTH HOUSE (FAR HORIZONS)
Ruler Pisces

The influence of Pisces further impels Cancer towards an interest in religion, the spiritual and the mystical. The house of dreams and imagination is ruled by the dreaming sign of Pisces; Cancers can often by intensely idealistic people. When things work, Cancer people can be utterly selfless altruists, giving all their compassion to the unhappy and dispossessed of life. The problem for them is, of course, practicality.

Because the ninth house always draws a person beyond themselves, and Pisces has a nebulous quality of yearning about it, Cancer people can need to express their idealism and altruism intensely. What they have to do is to sit down and consider just how to do it. 'What goals do I have, and what possible ways of going about them do I have? Who can help and in what ways? What negative consequences can there be – What might I neglect? *Who* might I neglect?' This exercise is certainly difficult for Cancer; Pisces is too dreamy a sign to be a good influence and its emotionality adds to Cancer's feeling-based, rather than thinking-based, approach to these things. Sometimes sheer intuitive understanding may lead Cancer to the right answer, but it's as well to analyse the intuition too! Cancer tends to overidealize principles and even people he believes in and they *have* to be subjected to analysis, whether it's a guru whose lofty teachings Cancer feels for or a charity Cancer is giving time to.

Often, the goal Cancer has may be intuitively right, and a worthwhile one, while it is the means which might be used to achieve the goal which Cancer is confused about or gets wrong. Cancer should concentrate on the practicalities of how to implement his nobler, humanitarian instincts.

TENTH HOUSE (CAREER)
Ruler Aries

Cancer people are very ambitious in their careers. The aggressive influence of Aries does harmonize with the general Cancer personality, because work is the main way of earning money in life for Cancer (as with everyone) and earning money, to guarantee security and give a feeling of self-worth, is essential to Cancer. So, getting on in one's career is of major importance to Cancer and the Aries energy really helps with this. Moreover, Cancer people can be quite tough and even ruthless about their careers. Anyone who is perceived as threatening the security of Cancer's career will be subjected to a violently aggressive and emotional crusade against them. Work is money is emotional security is the equation, so any threat to a career is a threat to Cancer's basic sense of self-worth. Cancer people are particularly responsive to those people in superior positions or ones of authority; harsh words from bosses make them very unhappy and they expect to be treated fairly. Which they should be; they work very hard, very fairly, are kindly to those working under them and expect such treatment from those placed over them.

Aries' influence also helps to overcome Cancer's natural introversion when it comes to career matters. Something in Cancer – this Aries influence – almost relishes a good bit of fair competition in his career life. A fair challenge is enjoyable for Cancer. Cancer people will particularly enjoy such challenges if placed in authority (Aries' influence) over a group of people working on a project, and they will be very good in such a role since they treat others very fairly. The natural aggression of Aries could make Cancer bossy, and it is possible that this will happen as a defensive reaction if Cancer feels threatened in some way or insecure, but usually Cancer's natural sensitivity to the feelings of others prevents this happening. Bossiness can be a problem for Cancer people, though, if they feel that they are bossing other people for their own good, because then the Cancer person feels that this is a protective way of treating people. It isn't, and this may be a problem Cancer people need to watch for. Benevolent dictatorship is still repression, no matter how good the intentions are.

ELEVENTH HOUSE (FRIENDSHIPS)
Ruler Taurus

In casual friendships, Cancer people are down-to-earth and practical. They like the company of practical people, and especially of wealthy people; they also like people who are stable, and have the earthy qualities of Taurus. The drawback is that Cancer folk, being somewhat introvert anyway, tend to be over-conservative and to stick with the friends they know well and trust. This can pay dividends for Cancer; they certainly need stable friends, because Cancer is naturally moody but is also responsive to the moods of others, so being in the company of stable people tends to stabilize Cancer's moods too. However, sometimes Cancer may miss career opportunities or picking up useful pieces of information because he avoids the unconventional or unusual people in his social circles. Still, it's the case that knowing wealthy people is often one of the ways in which Cancer people further their own careers. There's nothing calculating about this; it's a natural preference for Cancer.

Cancer is also drawn to elegant, artistic and beautiful or handsome people; qualities which the Taurus influence likes in others.

And Cancer is undoubtedly as affectionate to his friends as he is loving to his family, and is generous and hospitable to them (the Taurean influence again). Cancer people do not deceive or short-change their friends. Also, it's rare for Cancer to be deceived or cheated in return; partly because it would take a very mean specimen of humanity to do it at all and also partly because Taurus is a practical and slightly suspicious influence. Finally, Cancer is very sensitive to others and tends to pick up any hostile or deceitful feelings towards himself which others may harbour.

TWELFTH HOUSE (THE UNCONSCIOUS)
Ruler Gemini

The twelfth house concerns hidden things within the personality, that which isn't expressed easily; in this case, the logical thinking powers of Gemini. One facet of Gemini's influence is that Cancer children are often slown to develop their powers of reasoning; another is that Cancer adults may only find it easy to sit down and think things over (no matter what – career, family problems, almost anything) when alone. They need time to fathom things out, to go over everything involved slowly and carefully, and only then to discuss them with others or try their ideas out. Cancer people also keep their ideas secret in many cases; this goes hand in hand with the natural withdrawing, introvert tendencies of Cancer. Cancer people may spend a long time quietly making plans before discussing them or doing anything.

The Gemini influence also gives many Cancer people a strong craving for education and learning which doesn't end when schooldays are over. Many Cancer adults may attend night school classes, adult education centres or even do Open University courses. The twelfth house governs unconscious *needs*, and the need to develop the mind is one bequeathed by Gemini's influence. But also Gemini's influence may help Cancer in his emotional life; because Gemini almost makes the unconscious mind rational (if such a thing is possible), Cancer's intuitions may become increasingly accurate as he grows older. Gemini learns; and Cancer comes to know and understand things, especially about other people (Gemini's natural affinity), which are not easily put into words. Cancer has the general emotional responsiveness to others, and Gemini unconsciously analyses what's going on. This can lead to many Cancer adults being uncannily accurate in their understanding of others at an intuitive level.

Problems will arise for Cancer people if they rely solely on their emotional responsiveness to, and evaluation of, other people and don't satisfy the needs of the unconscious Gemini influence. This is why adult education, or simply reading books or watching films which have some educational content is an important activity for Cancer people. Another problem is that Cancer people may, under Gemini's promptings, blurt out things about their emotional life when they shouldn't, to listeners who may not treat them with the sympathy and caution they should. Gemini wants to communicate, after all. The need to think things out for oneself – alone – first of all, is very great in Cancer.

☆ ☆ ☆

Cancer people often do not have an easy passage in life. Their inner insecurities, the strength of their emotions and their sensitivity to others don't make for easy happiness. But at least when things are good for them, when they feel secure and loved and know that those they love are safe and well and love them in return, Cancer people can know a depth of happiness beyond most others. Cancer is a loving, generous and fair-hearted (I should say fair-minded, but this seems more appropriate for this sign) person, and the rest of us probably have more love and affection in our lives with them than we ever would without them.

Leo rising
THE LION

The proud and magnificent lion is the symbol for Leo, the 'royal' sign. Like the king of beasts, Leo is a proud, regal creature; great-hearted and generous. Leos are also great dominators of those around them, projecting their personalities powerfully, inviting others to admire and flatter them. Leos have many great merits; they are incapable of meanness or petty-mindedness, they are devoted to loved ones and friends – spite and malice are beneath them. But there is something else . . . suitably enough, lions don't actually do much hunting for food. It's the lionesses who do that for them. And both male and female Leos are more like lions than lion-esses in this respect. After all, doing things is somewhat below their dignity; they like to lie in the sun and enjoy themselves as lions do.

And, while Leo's powerful personality cannot be ignored, when you know a Leo they're more like kittens than great cats; indeed, rather like that soft kind of kitten that loves rolling over on its back and having its tummy rubbed. Leos are easily manipulated by others through flattery and are child's play to outwit. However, it would take a really mean person to do that to such a great-hearted and benevolent personality as a Leo. And Leos don't forget kind-nesses done for them; their memories are long and their devotion endless. They are friends beyond price.

The key components of Leo's general personality are *dominating* and *attention-seeking*; it isn't enough for Leo to be in charge, he must know that others *see* that he is a leader, and be recognized as such by them. These desires colour everything in Leo's life. This is because the 'Leo factor' here governs the first house, the general personality overlay; what is crucial to Leo is to be admired for himself, for the power and force of his personality.

SECOND HOUSE (MONEY)
Ruler Virgo

Leo will often make money by using his mind; the reasoning powers that Virgo brings to the affairs of this house. Leos do not often want to do such things as hard manual labour! Leos have the ability to be careful about money, and to budget wisely; again, Virgo's influence. But whether they do so is another matter. Leo is too generous to be thrifty and his general instinct is to spend freely, but the Virgo influence dislikes this. The solution for Leo is to keep back a certain percentage of what he earns – in a regular saving account of some kind – settle his regular bills likewise (in advance, preferably) and spend the rest as he wishes. This is the only way of allowing himself the impulse spending he wants to indulge in and also satisfying Virgo's demands for order and carefulness.

Leo is also careful about money when it's due to him; Leo is proud and won't be cheated, and while his pride might sometimes make him not wish to condescend to insist on fair treatment, Virgo won't be done out of what is rightfully its property and Leo is a stickler for fairness. Likewise Leo settles his debts fully – eventually.

Leo is advised *not* to enter into too many hire purchase agreements, not to collect too many credit cards and generally not to run up excessive debts. This is very easy for Leo if the debts are 'invisible' as they seem to be in these cases.

THIRD HOUSE (COMMUNICATING)
Ruler Libra

Now we can see part of the reason why Leo, although he is a dominator of other people, doesn't put other people's backs up. The Libran charm comes across in the way he communicates with other people. Leo is able to express himself gracefully, artistically with beautiful manners. He's a delight to listen to.

Leo also gains a useful skill from Libra; the sign of the balance makes Leo a good negotiator, almost a diplomat. He has the ability to balance different points of view and arrive at fair solutions to problems. If Leo feels himself to be in a safe position of authority, so that his ego feels secure, he can play this role to absolute perfection. Negotiations in politics, industrial relations and in almost any walk of life are happy hunting grounds for Leos.

There's also something of Libra's liking for luxury (hardly alien to Leo's general personality) connected with third house affairs. Leo will like writing on high-quality personal stationery, having the best typewriter he can afford (probably a better one that he can), possessing some preposterously ornate telephone and travelling in luxury. Leo often writes in flowing, mega-sized handwriting, florid but still graceful.

Libra's liking for partnership means that Leo will enjoy working with others to communicate ideas; writing together, working in a team in some way. And, of course, this influence increases Leo's natural gregariousness – he always wants an audience!

FOURTH HOUSE (HOME)
Ruler Scorpio

Leos are intense about their homes and families. Go near a litter of lion cubs and the lion growls very menacingly; when lions growl at you, you are advised to have a rapid means of exiting from the situation. Scorpio's intensity fuels Leo's drives to dominance; in a family with a Leo in it, there's never any doubt who wears the trousers around the place. This is as true of female Leos as it is of males.

Leo's dominance over his family can create problems if it's overdone; Leo's personality is so powerful that he can almost overwhelm other family members. His children may be so in awe of him that they almost fear him and can have problems developing their own identities. But his benevolence and generosity is endless, and eventually his family see the kitten beneath the great cat's façade. Leo children are a delight for their parents; they are very proud of their homes and families, but they can be exacting about them, and ashamed of them if they don't meet rather high standards!

Leo's home is usually a regal, opulent place. Leo's home base is somewhere where others are invited to admire Leo's powerful personality expressed through his possessions. *Always* flatter a Leo's home (after you have finished flattering Leo himself, of course). But there is always some secret part of it which Leo likes to keep for himself (the secretive side of Scorpio). It may be an attic, a study room, a basement, but somewhere around the place Leo needs his own den where he can work, relax and growl to no-one in particular. This is an important psychological need for Leo, and without it he can experience a vague sense of frustration about his life without knowing why.

Scorpio's sexual connection means that Leo often entertains his objects of affection in his home, preparing fine meals and serving fine wines or champagne; but not always. Being seen in public with an attractive partner (and being complimented on it afterwards) is pure delight for Leo.

FIFTH HOUSE (CREATIVITY)
Ruler Sagittarius

Leo is never short of ideas. How could he be, with the restless and endlessly inventive influence of the Centaur-Archer stimulating his creativity? Leo feels that there's nothing he can't do, given a little time. Ideas flow freely from him, about virtually everything imaginable. The general pride of the Leo personality, and the optimism and enthusiasm of Sagittarius, give Leo the feeling that all things are possible.

Leo's two problems are those of Sagittarius – a lack of application and some impracticality. Sagittarius doesn't want to have to knuckle down to one problem and concentrate on it for days, even when this has to be done. Sagittarius is too restless and gets bored easily; and the lion is a lazy beast at heart. Leo simply *has* to develop persistence. Things have to be done at certain times, and Leo has to use work rotas, or work deadlines, to make himself concentrate on things which have to be done, problems which have to be solved. This applies to almost everything in his life – finance, work, domestic budgets, anything where creative or applied, practical effort is needed.

Leo also needs to throw cold water over his own ideas by forcing himself to face up to practicalities. This is easier in some spheres than others – as we've seen, the influence of Virgo on the second house means that Leo does have the ability to plan financially reasonably carefully. Since Sagittarius is gregarious and virtually unoffendable, Leo should use other people as throwers of cold water if he can't somehow do it himself.

The fifth house also rules romance, and the Sagittarian influence is strong. Leo really is an incurable romantic; the lion really does believe that it will all turn out gloriously in the end, as he and his loved one disappear off into some sunlit exotic scene to partake of oysters and champagne and live happily (and luxuriously) ever after. It's nonsense, of course. Leo is a fine and loyal, proud and loving, partner but the Sagittarian influence means that he's restless. Leo's always looking elsewhere, and he's curious and stimulated by novelty for its own sake. He can be deeply loving and quite unfaithful at the same time. Potential partners need to know this!

Leo is impractical about romance and one major weakness in him is that he spends large sums on beautiful things for his loved one, far more than he can afford. Leo is generous and Sagittarius impulsive and neither of them cool-headed. Leo can virtually bankrupt himself for a lover. One way or another Leo will learn this lesson!

SIXTH HOUSE (WORK/SERVICE)
Ruler Capricorn

Leo's natural inclinations to laziness are countered here. Capricorn is a powerfully industrious influence, and when Leos work, they work hard. Moreover, they know what to do and how to do it; Capricorn is very practical and Leos are able to work efficiently and without wasting much time. They learn to find out the right ways of doing things quickly, usually from other people rather than from books or manuals or other teaching aids.

The effects of pressure of work on Leo are not predictable. Some Leo people, in whom the Capricorn influence is strong and benevolent, can work with amazing speed and efficiency under pressure; other Leos, where the Capricorn influence is weak, can crack up under pressure and usually avoid work if the pressure is on, thus making their problems even worse. It's essential for a Leo person who has problems with time pressures at work to arrange his schedule so that these problems do not arise, by trying to work flexible hours, trying to keep a little ahead of things by doing some routine work lying around when things are slack, delegating work and keeping careful written schedules of work loads. Otherwise, Leo can become utterly wretched and make himself unhappy and his workmates angry, thinking that he's shirking responsibility when he just can't face it.

Oddly enough, Capricorn's influence gives Leo the ability to tolerate for some time, mundane or tedious work, or something below his abilities or capacity for responsibility, if he sees that this can lead to better things in the future (Leo's pride needs that assurance). This is a fortunate thing for Leo; he wants to be the boss (or an executive at least) but one can't start out in that position! Leo should, if offered such a job, check potential promotion prospects carefully. It will make him feel much happier about what he's doing.

Likewise, Capricorn's influence gives Leo the ability to be of service to others, when this might seem very alien to the King of beasts. But, again, this must be for a limited time or only in a small area of his work or life.

Capricorn's robust nature gives Leo generally good health and he has good stamina and endurance. However, it is important for Leos to lead ordered lives to stay healthy; to make sure they get enough sleep, to eat properly and at the right times, and so on. That's true for most people but essential for Leo!

SEVENTH HOUSE (MARRIAGE/PARTNERSHIPS)
Ruler Aquarius

The Aquarian influence ensures that Leos like to be independent in partnerships; they don't like committing themselves fully to partnerships and although they are fair-minded their natural pride means that something within them always feels that they are the superior part of any partnership they're involved with. Leos are also prone to make sudden breaks in partnerships, particularly if their pride or independence is challenged or they feel themselves hemmed in.

The unconventional influence of Aquarius means that there is often something unusual or peculiar about business partnerships Leos are involved with – notably, they can be too offhand or informal about their involvements. Leos need to make sure that carefully scrutinized written contracts and the like are prepared when they enter into business arrangements. The pride of Leo ensures that delegating these matters to accountants or, more humbly, their spouses is not too difficult for them.

The same restless individualism and unconventionality applies to the marriages of Leos. As we've seen, they are romantic and stimulated by novelty and not too readily given to faithfulness in any case. Also, combined with Leo's pride, the Aquarian curiosity and need to know things makes them rather busybodying about their spouses. They want to know what they're doing all the time.

Although he himself is not usually faithful, Leo's pride demands that his partner should be. This double standard, applying to both male and female Leos, is obviously a likely source of problems for Leo and his partner. And a final problem is that Aquarius' rebellious nature may lure Leo into marriage for reasons of rebelling against family or convention; an error he can regret at his leisure. Leos should be very careful when considering marriage!

EIGHTH HOUSE (NEEDS FROM OTHERS)
Ruler Pisces

The Piscean influence *can* fuse with Leo's general benevolence and generosity to create an inspirational person, someone capable of expressing his need for altruism and his desire for a better life for humanity in general brilliantly and persuasively. Pisces is a dreamer and can bring this quality of inspiration. But while Pisces can be a positive influence on *what* Leo projects of his inner needs to others, it isn't a helpful influence when it comes to *how* Leo expresses himself. Pisces' difficulties in putting inspired ideas into coherent speech can produce a Don Quixote kind of person, a rambling and uncertain speaker, who seems only to have foolish idealistic beliefs lacking in practicality.

The Piscean influence on Leo's material needs and how these are satisfied by others is not a good one. Such things as inheritances, or money owed to Leo in other ways, can almost seem to melt away before Leo gets his paws on the loot; misfortune is often his lot.

As always with a Piscean influence, the problem for Leo is putting things in practical terms. Contracts, written agreements, careful consideration of what he wants and what he needs (not always the same thing), who can help, what's practically certain, what's possible and what's probably just a hopeful dream; these are essential for Leo.

NINTH HOUSE (FAR HORIZONS)
Ruler Aries

The powerful energies of Aries drive Leo into expressing those ideas which inspire him and take him beyond himself. Leo is intensely creative anyway, given Sagittarius' rulership of the fifth house, and the Piscean influence on the eighth house can also make him an altruist. So Leo has lots of ideas to express and Aries drives him onwards.

Leo functions excellently in any job where he is projecting ideas; promotions, advertising, salesmanship – even something as unusual as missionary work (the ninth house governs religious belief). But Leo will be projecting *his* ideas; Aries is very egotistical. If he's working for others, Leo is only expressing their views because he agrees with them and he will certainly add his own little riders to what he says or writes.

Leo is really a crusader for his ideas. He believes fervently that his views are right, and expresses them with unflagging energy. He might accept in argument that he *could* be wrong but in his heart he knows he isn't. Not only would Aries not brook such an idea but Leo's pride wouldn't accept it either. And this pinpoints a problem for Leo; he can be completely dogmatic in his beliefs. It is always an error to tell a Leo that he is wrong about something. The only way to change Leo's mind is to suggest that perhaps there is something more to the problem or idea he's talking about and has he considered such-and-such alternative possibilities? Now Leo will listen, but a flat contradiction will never get across to him.

TENTH HOUSE (CAREER)
Ruler Taurus

Leo is really quite humble about his career: all he wants is recognition and fame on the one hand (Leo's pride) and plenty of money too (Taurus' influence). Given the choice, it isn't easy, but Leo would probably plump for the money; Leo wants it to build his home base, to buy flamboyant and beautiful things to get himself admired and recognized. Leo wants to earn a lot to keep himself in the manner he'd like to be accustomed to and which he knows is his divine right.

Fortunately, Taurus is a very practical influence and Leos can be very determined and careful about building their careers. It doesn't have to be instant fame and fortune – Taurus is not too unhappy with taking things step by step – but there must be the clear possibility of fame and fortune in the distance. This fits with Capricorn's rulership of the sixth house; Leo can be patient in more junior or menial jobs but he must see the higher reaches opening up in the foreseeable future, or else he will get frustrated and irritable.

Leo is generally somewhat lazy but Taurus is hard-working and its influence means that Leo *can* work hard at his job – under the right conditions. Often, Leo will laze around for a while, then put in a burst of intense activity for a while, and then laze around some more. In fact, this isn't a good way for him to work; it can lead to health problems or bad moods. As we saw when looking at the sixth house, Leo should try to order his work life into a regular pattern.

ELEVENTH HOUSE (FRIENDSHIPS)
Ruler Gemini

Gemini's influence is happily in harmony with Leo's general personality. The Gemini influence leads Leo to seek out lots of friends, preferably those who are witty and fast-thinking and express ideas cleverly. Leo likes the company of such people, to stimulate his own ideas and creativity. Leo generally has many circles of relatively superficial acquaintances; there is likely to be a clear division in Leo's mind between the circles of acquaintances he has and his intimate friends. There are no half-way cases.

Leo cannot abide boring people; what he's after is mental stimulation above everything else. Small talk is only all right if it's witty and mentally quick; Leo likes verbal riddles, puns and the like.

Gemini's influence pinpoints an important need which Leo has: he does need others to express ideas to, to get their reactions and develop his ideas through discussion and feedback. Now, since Leo is often dogmatic about his central views on life, people and whatever work he's most occupied with, this may not be so easy. But Leo *has* to have other people to bounce ideas off; he will not be able to test his ideas (especially against the practicalities of life) on his own.

TWELFTH HOUSE (THE UNCONSCIOUS)
Ruler Cancer

One of the effects of Cancer's influence is to reinforce a tendency in Leo which Scorpio's rulership of the fifth house gives him; Leo needs a place to himself, a 'hidden' place in his own home (Cancer being the sign of the home) where he can contemplate those ideas within himself which he cannot express so easily. Alone, he needs his ideas to flow from his unconscious; doing nothing, just letting them come to him, considering them later (and discussing them with friends, as we've just seen).

Cancer's influence gives Leo a vulnerability which is not often seen by others. He hides hurts he gets from rejections or belittlements by others; his pride won't let him show his hurt, but Cancer feels it, and he retreats off alone to lick his wounds. It also gives Leo a darker side; Leo does not forget a hurt. Cancer hoards up emotional hurts in Leo's unconscious and a bitter Leo, his pride offended and his emotions hurt, can make a relentless and unmerciful enemy.

If Leo is out of circulation for a while, you know the lion is licking his wounds for some reason, so don't approach him. Biblical characters may have been able to handle lions with thorns in their paws but the rest of us will get our heads bitten off.

Because the twelfth house indicates what it is that a person often finds it hardest to express, Cancer's rulership shows that Leo may find it hard to show his compassion or maternal instincts to, and for, other people. He may seem unfeeling sometimes; the truth of it is that he may find someone else's hurt too painful to talk about because his Cancer unconscious makes him acutely aware of it on an intuitive level. Moreover, the proud lion is not readily seen crying or showing similar reactions.

Finally, Cancer ruling the twelfth can make Leo acutely sensitive to criticism. He hardly seems to be, but wise friends know to criticize his ideas gently even if he is being rather dogmatic about things!

☆ ☆ ☆

Leo's failings really are pretty trivial when compared with his positive qualities. He's generous to a fault, devoted and loyal, and he never forgets a friend. All he wants in return is a little admiration and flattery. You only have to *pretend* that he's the king of the coop, after all.

Virgo rising
THE VIRGIN

Careful, logical and precise, Virgo is a cool-headed creature. Virgo is an intellectual; he analyses, thinks things through, and is attentive to all the small details of problems other people miss. Virgo has an enquiring and critical mind, and loves knowledge for its own sake; but Virgo often hides behind his strong mind, quoting other people's ideas or interrogating others rather than expressing himself in any forthright way.

Just as Virgo loves fine detail, he loves precision and order and cleanliness. Virgo has everything just so, in its right place, probably labelled, filed, cross-indexed and filled in in triplicate. These abilities give Virgo the potential to go a long way in his chosen career.

But Virgo is a cool customer; the symbol of the virgin shows us that. Virgo is not carried away by emotions and can be quite a dry, unfeeling person. Virgo can be something of a bore sometimes – but on the other hand his vast store of knowledge of all kinds of unlikely things and small points of detail can make him a fascinating person to listen to. If he chooses to hold forth!

The general personality overlay for Virgo is *love of order* and *perfectionism*. Virgo strives for quality over quantity at all times, and his work and ways of expressing himself are precise and correct. Virgo's critical nature can make him quite a harsh person at times, but this may spring from an inner sense of inferiority rather than from malice or meanness.

SECOND HOUSE (MONEY)
Ruler Libra

At once we see part of the reason why Virgo is a superb ledger-keeper; the sign of the balance governs the house of money. Virgo is absolutely meticulous in keeping accounts. He has drawers full of receipts for things he bought years ago, and he probably carries round a mental list of them all too (which he can recall in either alphabetical or chronological order!).

Libra's socializing influence means that Virgo tends to earn money primarily through working with other people; obviously, that's true for most of us, but with Virgo the connection may be with an especially close friend or a husband or wife (Libra's association with close partnerships). Also, Libra's association with artistic and beautiful things gives Virgo the ability to acquire money through affairs connected with such things – which can be anything from designing clothes to being a florist.

The problem for Virgo is that secretly he wants to be rather extravagant in his spending on beautiful things; Libra wants cosseting. This can work out if Virgo allows himself small occasional expenditure on little things which please him; Libra is not a lover of opulence as such and little things beautifully made please Virgo. It can be a small brooch, an ornament for the home, a well-made fountain pen – something like this; Virgo will do well to budget a little for a small extravagance like this on a regular basis. Without this, Libra will grow unhappy and frustrated and Virgo may become depressed, feeling that there's something missing from his life and that everything is rather grey and drab. This may end up in an impulsive spending spree, which Virgo will regret for months afterwards! It ruins the accounts.

THIRD HOUSE (COMMUNICATING)
Ruler Scorpio

Now this really is intriguing. Virgo is well known as a mentally powerful but somewhat retiring person. Yet here's the sign of powerful energy ruling the house of communicating. Why isn't Virgo a real trail-blazer, an incessant talker and conversationalist? Because he usually isn't.

What Scorpio gives Virgo is the ability to think incisively, to get to the bottom of problems and see all the angles. Scorpio's energy with Virgo's thoroughness is a powerful mix. And it also gives Virgo the ability to persuade others through argument; Virgo's logic is good but the magnetic quality of Scorpio gives him that extra persuasive edge. But there is always something secretive and hidden about Scorpio; and this influence tends to make Virgo (who is rather introverted anyway) prefer to develop his ideas on his own and keep them to himself. He will use the power of his mind to analyse and criticize others, but he will not give himself away easily. He is brief, precise and frank in what he says, but Scorpio keeps something back to mull over in private.

Still, Scorpio's power gives Virgo strong energies in communicating and this is something he may easily exploit in his career, working in television, video, radio, journalism or any field where communication skills are important. But rather than being an actor, say, he would prefer to be a producer, working away behind the scenes rather than putting himself up front.

Virgos also find well-argued cases from others particularly pleasing, almost as if the person who takes the time to argue carefully with them is paying them a compliment. Someone who supports Virgo's case with his own arguments is likely not to be forgotten in a hurry!

FOURTH HOUSE (HOME)
Ruler Sagittarius

Virgo's home base will be an interesting place given the Sagittarian influence. Virgo wants an expansive, large home. It doesn't have to be luxurious, but there has to be lots of space. It will be packed with things which are food for Virgo's mind; TV, radio, video, and above all books, thousands of them. Virgo likes to retire to his home base and think and learn, devouring information about everything.

There may be a degree of organized chaos about Virgo's home. Books and papers will be everywhere, in bookcases standing at improbable angles against each other, and seemingly all over the place. But Virgo knows just where everything is. Even if his home is untidy (Sagittarius must be the untidiest sign in the Zodiac, but Virgo's general love of order may overrule this influence), the odds are that Virgo will have periodic bouts of filing and re-ordering everything and his home is *never* dirty.

Virgos are generous hosts in their homes; Sagittarius' influence ensures that. Their dinner parties are great if you can handle the conversation afterwards; the coffee is accompanied by Virgo starting the intellectual cross-questioning. This can be hard work. At the very least Virgo wants to hear some gossip and to know what you think about everything from the space shuttle to the educational TV programme he watched last night.

Virgos are also generous towards their families, and kindly and fair with them. Domestic harmony is usually the revailing state of affairs in Virgo's home (Sagittarius' benign influence). If there is a problem, it may be connected with some coolness of emotions; Virgo and Sagittarius are both 'mental' signs and neither is given to frequent expression of emotion. It's crucial to remember that the way to a Virgo's heart is through his head – thus, parents of a Virgo child will please him and win his affection by giving him gifts of books or a home computer he can use for learning or by simply telling him stories. If it feeds Virgo's mind, his affections are won over.

FIFTH HOUSE (CREATIVITY)
Ruler Capricorn

How well Capricorn's influence fits with Virgo's general personality! When Virgo is daydreaming or developing his ideas, they're always practical. Virgo has an intuitive sense of how to make things work for him in what he's doing, whether it's at home or at work or anywhere else. Virgo almost doesn't have to *try* to put his inspirations into practical form; they just come to him that way anyway. This saves a lot of time! But it also makes Virgo very conservative. True originality is almost unheard of with Virgo; most of his insights are just twists on existing ideas rather than anything new. But that is Virgo's place in the scheme of things; he is the careful practical developer, the person who makes things work, neatly and precisely, like clockwork. The dreaming can be left to others.

Where Capricorn's influence is not so fortunate is on Virgo's romantic life. Virgos are rather prudish about sex, which makes life tricky for them because they really don't lack libido; the goat is hardly given to chastity, despite the symbol used for Virgo. And Virgos often make a cardinal error in romance by choosing someone they feel *needs* them; need is not so good a basis for a relationship. There may be a degree of inequality in Virgo's relationships, and Virgos are afraid of losing control over themselves and their emotions. And Capricorn's very down-to-earth, no-

nonsense influence almost kills the spirit of romance in some Virgo people. This isn't an easy sign for the romantic!

Capricorn's influence spreads more widely from romance to generally pleasurable activities; Virgos take their pleasures seriously and many of them seem old before their time, having a grave and serious outlook – almost being kill-joys. Yet Virgo does have sensual drives, if he can only allow himself the room to express them. This will always be a major problem for Virgo and there is no simple answer to it.

SIXTH HOUSE (WORK/SERVICE)
Ruler Aquarius

Virgo likes work routines that are suited to him, rather than designed for others; he's rather stubborn about this. Virgo has his own way of doing things, given the individualistic Aquarius influence, and that's how he wants to get on with his work. He works happily enough with others – Aquarius is sociable enough – but really he prefers to do the essential things on his own. And this is really crucial for him, for if he isn't allowed to use his own original methods of working, Aquarius' rebellious instincts will come to the fore and Virgo will get very shirty indeed.

The influence of Aquarius can be very positive, because the originality of the sign coupled with Virgo's meticulous nature gives Virgo the ability to think of an insightful approach to some work project and then really see it through. But as often as not, what happens is that Virgo may be tempted to flit from one thing to another at work, doing 90% of each important thing and then leaving some last little detail unattended to. This is Aquarius at its most negative, and Virgo will wonder what streak of contrariness in himself makes this happen, because he really isn't like this at all. Careful planning of work schedules will help a lot here.

Health-wise, Aquarius may make Virgo a rather cranky health faddist; Virgo is fastidious enough as it is. He may be a great popper of every type of vitamin pill on the market, fond of herbal remedies and alternative healing treatments. It won't do him any harm but he may get rather boring about it! What Virgo should avoid given the Aquarian influence is any over-indulgence in drink or drugs, which will harm his health badly. This is an important point for Virgos to watch out for.

SEVENTH HOUSE (MARRIAGE/PARTNERSHIPS)
Ruler Pisces

Pisces' influence might seem to undermine Virgo here; after all, Virgo is careful and meticulous and Pisces is disorganized and dreamy. Quite often, what happens is that Virgos are attracted to people who are less organized than they are. They like taking over responsibility for ordering the lives of their partners and close friends – which gives them a reputation for bossiness. But, likewise, rather disorganized people can find the close friendship of Virgos very helpful to them and the attraction can be mutual.

With the nebulous quality of Pisces, Virgos often take over the running of the day-to-day affairs of their marriages and close partnerships without the partner actually realizing fully what's going on, in all sorts of little ways which escape the attention of other people.

A trap for Virgo is to be unrealistic in marriage and partnership – the classic problem for a Piscean influence. They may put their loved ones on a pedestal, over-idealizing them, and they may expect far too much from them. Likewise, Virgos should be very careful with business partnerships, since the Piscean influence makes them unrealistic about these too; they should check carefully as to whether what they're hoping for is really practically possible. Pisces' influence only makes worse Virgo's desire for perfection in things.

If Virgo is disappointed in a close partnership it may be very hard for him to recover; he distrusts his feelings and perceptions in such matters and may become a rather embittered loner. That comes across in a heightening of his critical, carping side, and it's generally easy to recognize a Virgo of this type.

EIGHTH HOUSE (NEEDS FROM OTHERS)
Ruler Aries

The Aries influence on the Virgo person is very double-edged. It *can* give Virgo the drive and push to express his needs clearly to others (the Aries drive; the Virgo ability to express himself clearly and concisely) so that Virgo doesn't go begging for money and resources. But Aries is an aggressive influence and Virgo can be too argumentative, too critical and carping in the way he comes across.

Virgo may have quarrels about money, particularly where joint finances are concerned. In extreme cases this can even end up in M'learned friends being called in. Likewise, Virgo can expect aggressive and irritable responses from other people if he doesn't express himself carefully. A Virgo thinking of asking for a pay rise should think long and hard about how he's going to argue his case.

Virgo needs to cool down about his financial needs. Because Libra rules the second house of a person with Virgo rising, the odds are that Virgo's earning capacities are always strongly connected with group work and he *can* be reasonable and diplomatic about his needs. What he *must* avoid is any impulsive arguing and any expression of his needs which he hasn't thought out coolly before-hand. This might seem an easy problem to avoid for Virgo, but in his monetary needs – well, this is the one area of life where he can be betrayed by over-impulsiveness.

NINTH HOUSE (FAR HORIZONS)
Ruler Taurus

Now we see another reason why Virgo isn't really one of nature's originators or inventive geniuses. Taurus' influence on the house of imagination is severely practical and down-to-earth. But it's not a negative influence by any means; Virgo's philosophy of life is practical indeed and he has a strong liking for the artistic and beautiful. Virgo admires precision, practically useful ideas and elegance.

Virgos likewise have very straightforward and rather black-and-white views on social problems, politics and religion. They don't change their ideas easily, and since their powers of argument are pretty formidable it isn't easy to change their minds on such matters. In some cases, Virgo can really be quite bigoted; a lot will depend on his upbringing. Virgo can also be quite carping and unsympathetic to dreams and people who want to change the world for the better; their hearts may be in the right place but that's not what interests Virgo. For Virgo, if it doesn't look like working out pretty quickly it really isn't worth thinking about. Virgo takes a rather short-term approach to things and wants results quickly. Anything else is a waste of time.

If Virgo can use his imaginative abilities, it's in connection with anything beautiful or artistic (Taurus' influence). But even here it's likely that Virgo will dream up something well in line with ideas that already exist, simply expressing these in a slightly different way or maybe somehow capturing the basics of an idea in his imagination: there's always something pleasing to Virgo in a clean, efficient construction.

Virgo needs to be more patient with dreamers. Virgo should hold off from being too critical about such people; he should learn to guide them gently towards more practical expression of their ideas by asking them gently how their dreams might be put into practice. If he can do this, Virgo can be very helpful in stimulating other people's creativity.

TENTH HOUSE (CAREER)
Ruler Gemini

Gemini's influence really helps Virgo along in his career. Virgo likes any work which involves expressing ideas and getting them across to other people, and this is exactly what the Gemini influence gives him the ability to do. The other effect of Gemini's influence, of course, is to give Virgo more than one string to his bow. Virgo people usually have more than one type of work involvement at any one time, and the odds are that all of them involve working with other people to get some message across to others.

Virgo *must* have mental stimulation from his career. Virgo's mind craves this, and the Gemini influence demands it too. Virgo people simply *cannot* afford to work at any job where they do not meet mental challenges and don't have to think quickly. If their job doesn't demand this of them, they grow bored and restless (the Gemini influence again). However, they also need to be able to have some time alone to get their ideas clear, and they may not always express themselves at once when ideas do come to them (Scorpio's rulership of the third house). This makes Virgo a formidable worker; he's fast on the uptake mentally and given the chance to think things over for a while his ideas are even more powerfully right than his original reactions.

For a Virgo person, stimulation and variety at work are *essential*. A well-paid but dull job should be avoided at all costs; better a more modestly paid but exciting one.

ELEVENTH HOUSE (FRIENDSHIPS)
Ruler Cancer

We can see another reason why Virgo isn't always at once forth-coming with his ideas in conversation. Cancer is a retiring influence and it makes Virgo rather cautious with casual friends and acquaintances. Virgo is actually remarkably sensitive in his day-to-day dealings with such people, and can take offence very easily at minor slights in conversation. This is unfortunate for him, since Virgo's powerful mind and slightly critical nature mean that he can throw out verbal darts at others quite easily. When he gets them back, he is hypersensitive to them. It doesn't help that Virgo tends to be rather more attached emotionally to casual friends than others, given Cancer's influence. So Virgo can find what would be superficial relationships a bit more demanding than other people – so he may tend to avoid them to some extent. Virgo may retire behind the scenes to work his ideas out and communicate with others indirectly. And yet Cancer would really like to bring those friends into the home, almost as if they were members of Virgo's own family.

Although he is rather cool emotionally, Virgo can be a very sympathetic friend, given Cancer's influence. More than that; he can combine sympathy with a cool view of a person's problems given the analytical quality of his mind. Even with casual friends Virgo has the ability to understand difficulties and give good advice – he should be listened to, because with Cancer's influence he is sensitive to what's happening and his advice is sound and practical. Virgos can make very good friends indeed, if one understands that they may be more sensitive than they seem behind their rather cool and even critical exterior.

TWELFTH HOUSE (THE UNCONSCIOUS)
Ruler Leo

Now this really is a difficult business for Virgo. The Leo factor is the deepest drive in the personality, a compelling force, and Leo governs the house of hidden things, those things most difficult to express and come to terms with. This is a tricky combination.

Virgo may have enormous difficulty in coming to terms with a sense of pride, creativity and fulfilment. Virgo dimly senses that there may be something great and powerful within him but he doesn't know what. Virgo would like to be remembered for his genius but the Leo drive is more basic, more emotional, and Virgo cannot consciously grasp what is going on here. There are two possible reactions to this.

One way Virgo can go is to spend much time alone developing this unconscious force. The twelfth house forces are always most easily dealt with in solitude. Alone, Virgo begins to draw from within himself the power which fuels his ideas; he can finally begin to put together the pieces of the jigsaw. He may come up, at last, with some truly stunning idea of real originality. This obviously strengthens Virgo's need to retire from the world periodically – and as we've seen there are enough reasons for that already.

The other possible outcome is less fortunate. The Leo influence can give Virgo a secret feeling of superiority over other people; his deep pride makes him feel that others are inferior or even largely worthless. There are enough influences (like Taurus' rulership of the ninth house) on Virgo of this type already and if this happens Virgo can be little short of a monster.

What Virgo has to do is to come to terms with his pride. This is the major task in life for any Virgo, given the potency of Leo and the difficult nature of anything connected with the twelfth house. It is never an easy task. The first step is to realize the tremendous depth of willpower Leo's rulership of the twelfth house can bring, and to understand what this means. The next step is to think long and hard about how this willpower and mental force can be used together; what problems really stimulate these together? And what problems can I be working on which satisfy me and are useful and helpful to others? That's Virgo's job in life, and it will never be finally completed. When one thing is done, there must be something else for him.

☆ ☆ ☆

Virgo may not be blessed with the kindest heart of all, but he has enough sensitivity within him, and the power of his intellect is formidable indeed. He makes a surprisingly good friend for the rest of us if we can learn not to take his criticisms too personally (they aren't meant that way; it's the *ideas* that he is criticizing) and if we can argue carefully with him. You have to *work* to earn Virgo's friendship and affections.

Libra rising
THE BALANCE

The symbol of the balance shows us everything about Libra's prime need as a person. Both within himself and around himself — particularly where other people are concerned — Libra wants harmony, peace and fairness. The two are intimately connected with each other for Libra; he can only find a sense of peace and tranquillity within himself if his surroundings are peaceful and relaxed, with everything in balance. His natural sense of balance gives him a perfect sense of beauty and grace; Libra is a charming and fastidious person and has excellent taste.

Libra has the marvellous gift of being able to see all sides of arguments. Libra can always understand the other person's point of view. And Libra always wants agreements to be reached; strife and discord he can't stand. He's very sociable, loving the company of others, and dislikes being alone.

But, above all, Libra's great vice is laziness. Libra simply *hopes* that all will be sweetness and light and fairness in life and he's not usually prepared to work for it. He almost seems to think that a pleasant life is his natural birthright. Libra will usually avoid problems rather than dealing with them, if it's possible. When he is finally forced to deal with problems, it may be too late. In fact, Libra is rarely very good at dealing with his problems alone, and needs other people for advice and help.

Libra's general personality is shown by the symbol for the sign: the *need for balance* is what dominates Libra's life, in the affairs of all the other 11 houses.

SECOND HOUSE (MONEY)
Ruler Scorpio

The power of Scorpio gives Libra the potential to be a real money-winner. It gives him great earning potential. However, it's likely that Libra will get money not steadily all the time, but rather in large sums now and then. Libra needs to make careful budget plans to take care of this. Librans should avoid building up 'invisible' debts with credit cards, hire purchase agreements and the like; they're prone to doing this and it will be an error they can go on regretting for years as they struggle to pay off the debts.

Libra also has to be scrupulously honest about money. Scorpio is a secretive and, at worst, scheming and manipulating influence on Libra. Librans who enter into secret dealings with money may find that things end up very badly for them. Since Librans often get money from partners, the help of other people is a useful way of avoiding any tendencies to do this.

While Libra can earn a great deal of money, Libra isn't actually interested in money as such. He's more interested that the wealth he has is aesthetically pleasing in some way and he will use it to buy delightful things, or invest it in artistic possessions or projects or something similar. Libra wants money for the fair and delightful things it can buy. Libra is also generous with close friends and partners, and actually feels as if what is his is theirs too. He is generous to a fault in such matters.

THIRD HOUSE (COMMUNICATING)
Ruler Sagittarius

Libra's desire to be with people and to seek harmony and beauty in their presence is strongly reinforced by Sagittarius ruling this house. Sagittarius is gregarious, enthusiastic and a lover of fairness, and its influence makes Libra a talkative, versatile and fascinating person to be with. Sagittarius' enthusiasms and Libra's gracefulness make for a fast-talking, delightful speaker who gestures freely, laughs a lot and is generally great to be with. What's more, Sagittarius' interest in philosophy, religion and social affairs gives Libra something worth talking about. Libra really does want to teach the world to sing in perfect harmony, as the tired cliché of a certain soft drink advert puts it. And Libra is forever optimistic about it; Libra has a natural buoyancy, a real reserve of good spirits, when talking to other people. When Librans feel blue they can always make themselves feel better by meeting other people; this brings Sagittarius' good spirits into play and Libra feels happy again.

What's more, Sagittarius' inventiveness gives Libra the ability to be a natural problem-solver when dealing with other people. Since Libra wants to see those problems solved, this should work out well. But often it doesn't. Libra is lazy and Sagittarius lacks persistence. Libra may try to solve problems but not give the effort to see things through. What Librans should try to do is to cut down the number of personal problems they are getting involved with and to isolate the ones they think they can do the most about, figure out carefully how to go about it (Sagittarius has the resourcefulness to do that) and then make sure they *do* see things through. Continuous effort will certainly be more difficult for them than short-term, intensive bursts of activity and they should take that into account.

The third house also rules short-range travel and Librans like such journeys, given Sagittarius' restlessness. Regular weekend car-trips or train journeys, usually to see friends, can be an important source of pleasure in Librans' lives.

FOURTH HOUSE (HOME)
Ruler Capricorn

Capricorn's influence makes Librans surprisingly well-organized so far as their homes are concerned. Perhaps it's not so surprising after all; Capricorn's liking for having things in their right place harmonizes with Libra's liking for balance, beauty and his rather fastidious nature. Librans are great household organizers and their homes are unusually clean, well decorated and efficiently laid out. They are usually fairly lavishly decorated with ornaments, wall hangings and other beautiful things, but it's usually in good taste: Libra has that in abundance and Capricorn dislikes frivolity and excess. Capricorn's influence also makes Libra a better household worker than his general laziness might lead one to expect! Yet nothing is ever organized *quite* right for Libra. He's too perfectionistic about his home.

With their families, Capricorn can make Libra surprisingly disciplinarian. Libra is fair and just, and likes domestic harmony, but here he really won't take any nonsense. Libran parents can be rather stern with their children sometimes. But their sense of fairness stops them ever being cruel or mean towards them.

Libran children often have a rather stern, limiting upbringing. Capricorn brings this to bear in early life. This can be in any one (or more) of a variety of ways — a poor family, stern or harsh parents or parents separated in early life. Libran children are very sensitive to any anxieties or conflict in their families and wounds from such hurts can persist for many years.

Lastly, Capricorn's industrious influence often leads Libra to do much of his or her professional work at home, and indeed this is a good environment to work in. But only part of the time; Libra wants and needs the influence and advice of other people too much for that!

FIFTH HOUSE (CREATIVITY)
Ruler Aquarius

Aquarius gives Libra the ability to be truly ingenious and inventive in his work and thinking. Libra can see new ways of creating things which bring together existing ideas or things in new ways; they're really inventive. Oddly enough, Libra can work very effectively with new technologies, given the Aquarian influence. But Aquarius is gregarious just like Libra, and Libra will want to develop his ideas with or at least play his ideas off other people.

Libra will often involve himself with something, or someone, unusual in his creative endeavours. It's simply impossible to pigeon-hole how this works, given the influence of Aquarius. The only thing one can be sure of is that developing his creativity with other people is a *must* for Libra.

In romance, Libra is unconventional, and likes exciting and unusual involvements. Librans need drama and some flamboyance in their affairs, and are attracted to unusual people. They are often rebellious about their loves, and may have an affair with someone mostly because it scandalizes their parents or friends. The perverse quality of Aquarius makes this a possibility. Librans are charming and affectionate lovers, but the depth of their attachments is pretty doubtful. Aquarius never gave its heart to anyone, and Libra likes socializing too widely to be entirely happy with one person. For the partner of a Libran, giving the Libran plenty of rope and free time is important, and especially flattery about how lovely and graceful they are and how much one adores their clothes, jewellery, perfume, hairstyle, and so on is vital. Next to Leos, Librans love flattery more than any other Zodiac sign!

SIXTH HOUSE (WORK/SERVICE)
Ruler Pisces

The Piscean influence means that Libra *must* have an idealistic reason for the work he's doing. At the very least, he must feel he's developing as a person from doing it, and really he wants to do things which are useful to others. Artistic involvements are perfect for Libra; Pisces likes this too, and it is the ideal job for any Libran. Pisces' influence also makes Librans very sympathetic to the people they work with, and they want to help them; but their advice may not always be very good. Again, Libra needs to limit his involvement with these problems and think carefully about the practical side of dealing with just some of them.

The rather disorganized Pisces influence can bring Libra several problems. First, he may be hopelessly unrealistic about his work, hoping for some impossibly noble way of serving humanity through what he's doing. And he may take on more work than he can handle, and lose track of things; he can also lack the determination to complete work projects. Librans need to watch these points carefully. Finally, the sixth house rulership of health is important: for Libra, his physical health is usually bound up with his state of mind. In his work, organization is essential or else the Libran will suffer nervous complaints, and depression or a feeling of exhaustion. Libra often becomes ill because his nerves make him ill, and he should recognize this problem.

SEVENTH HOUSE (MARRIAGE/PARTNERSHIPS)
Ruler Aries

Librans can actually be quite aggressive and pushy when they want to enter partnerships affecting business, and even in friendships. They can be quite dominating, and they have the ability to spur other people into action in joint ventures, although they often don't realize this. Aries gives Libra that extra edge of energy, that pushiness which overcomes his natural laziness. They're also remarkably demanding of close friends and associates; they want to see an effort being put into the collaboration by their partner. One has to work surprisingly hard to please a Libran!

In their close friendships and marriages, Librans are quite dominating. They would often deny this, because they don't always do it in obvious ways. Despite the aggressive quality of Aries, Libra will often manipulate others by charm, diplomacy and persuasion. Libra will smooth-talk you into doing what he wants. And he does know what he wants, deep down.

However, sometimes the Aries energy works the other way round, and instead of becoming what Libra himself uses in his close relationships, it's what he seeks in his partner. He wants his inner aggressiveness reflected in that partner. There are Librans of both types, but in either case Libra tends to be involved with close partnerships which have some inequality in the dominance– submission stakes. Rather contrary for someone who likes a sense of balance and fairness, one might think, but then Libra probably feels that the balance between the two partners is the important thing. If he agreed there *was* an imbalance; often he'd deny it!

EIGHTH HOUSE (NEEDS FROM OTHERS)
Ruler Taurus

Taurus brings to Libra the ability to express his needs in straight-forward, down-to-earth ways. It's a very easily done thing for Libra; if the need is a material one (money and the like), well, Taurus is very concerned with such things and Libra is a graceful talker so matters aren't tricky. And with more emotional needs, Taurus is a practical influence. Libra knows how to express himself without making a meal of it.

Likewise, Libra tends to get straightforward and honest responses from others. Libra's plain speaking in such matters tends to make other people frank with him. Libra can be particularly gifted at extracting money from other people with his charm and practical ways of asking. As a fund-raiser for charity or good causes Libra is unequalled. It is also a talent which he can use in business, particularly with business associates he knows moderately well.

There's always likely to be something a little luxurious about Libra's way of expressing his material needs to others, and how these are fulfilled; Libra likes a little luxury and Taurus is no stranger to it. It may just be in the flourishes of his speech and gestures, or it may be the expensive lunch (hopefully on expenses) he gives a business friend to do some dealing!

NINTH HOUSE (FAR HORIZONS)
Ruler Gemini

Gemini's rulership of this house complements Libra's general personality in one way; Libra likes balancing and agreements and Gemini can always see both sides of an argument. Since this Gemini quality affects the house of imagination, of aspirations beyond oneself, we can see that Libra is prepared to consider all sides of arguments even about quite profound issues. Librans are rarely dogmatic about anything. On the other hand, they may never make their minds up about anything either. Gemini wants to know so much, to think everything over, to analyse and reflect, and in accord with Libra's laziness this can become a liking for thinking everything over and never quite deciding on anything.

And yet – Gemini is practical enough in many ways. Librans are great day-dreamers but Gemini wants things to be clear and logical, even if they are the products of the imagination. So, even though Librans may not be very decisive, they can be excellent at getting others to put their inspirations into practical form by cross-questioning them. And these matters interest Libra; Gemini always wants stimulation and interesting things to think about and its motivation won't be kept quiet for long. Libra wants, and likes, to talk about politics, society, religion, philosophy and the wider issues of the day; he may not hold views on such things with burning intensity (save for his love of justice and fairness) but he can be excellent at quietly persuading others to justify their beliefs. This makes him a valuable catalyst for the ideas of others.

TENTH HOUSE (CAREER)
Ruler Cancer

Cancer's influence gives Libra great sensitivity in his career and, more widely, about his public reputation. There are two important things about Libra's work, no matter what it is: first, he likes to work from home, at least a little. Cancer's influence ensures that. If it isn't professional work – which it will be if Libra can possibly arrange it – it'll be some kind of homework, or paperwork, connected with his job. Libran children may well be happier with homework than they are with schoolwork, if for some reason they aren't completely happy with the school they're in.

The other effect of Cancer's influence is that Libra likes working with groups where his role is somehow protective or maternal. A job where Libra is caring for others makes him feel a better person and satisfies his altruism. But a caring job which involves a lot of getting the hands dirty won't please Libra much; he's too fastidious for that.

Libra is kindly and protective to other people he's working with, especially younger people. Libra's a real sucker for anyone with big brown eyes and a helpless look. But it makes Libra greatly liked by his workmates, and especially by juniors who have the good fortune to be working for him. And, of course, Libra is always fair and just and wants to resolve conflicts between the people he works with. A Libran boss or work colleague makes life a great deal happier at work.

ELEVENTH HOUSE (FRIENDSHIPS)
Ruler Leo

The Leo factor ruling this house drives Libra outwards, towards others, and can operate in two ways. On the one hand, Libra is very proud of his friendships, and he needs to have many friends. But he does not dominate them, as you might expect from Leo's regal influence; rather, it tends to work the other way around. Libra is drawn to people who have Leo qualities; strong, dominant, creative people. Libra isn't necessarily submissive in their company but he almost seems to draw strength from them. The Leo factor in a Libran almost seems to work in reverse; it isn't so much a source of strength and a powerful drive within him so much as a need to draw strength from his friends. Libra *needs* his friends very deeply. And Libra is also very sensitive about even casual friendships. There are two reasons for that. The general Libra personality cannot abide conflicts and wants friendships to be harmonious affairs; and the Leo influence has its pride hurt if a friend rejects him. So Libra can tend to be unrealistic about friendships. He wants them to be plain sailing and yet he often doesn't make any effort to avoid problems that are building up (Libra and Leo are both somewhat inclined to laziness here) and neither does he make any effort to deal with problems when they come to the surface. Yet he still feels as if it's his right to have many happy and smiling friends!

An important point for Librans is that the rulership of the eleventh house by the creative sign Leo means that their creative efforts may often involve working with others. Since Pisces' rulership of the sixth house can make Librans somewhat unrealistic about work, this shows how to solve a problem: Librans should always be developing their ideas with others, because often they seem to develop greater creativity and power within themselves from being with creative and brilliant people.

TWELFTH HOUSE (THE UNCONSCIOUS)
Ruler Virgo

Libra is a sunny personality, on the surface. He seems to sail blithely along, not too worried by anything, getting by without being too brilliant or ultra-practical. But inside him there's a nagging little voice which wants to dot the i's and cross the t's. Now Libra doesn't want any of this. Libra wants to avoid complications, difficulties and all the fine-grain detail of things. And he finds it hard to sit down and be very analytical and think things out in detail when he has problems. He'd rather avoid them if possible.

Because the logical, planning quality of Virgo is a hard thing for Libra to draw out of himself, Librans often fail to accomplish things because they fail to look at the small print or check the minor practical details which can make all the difference. And yet they are aware of the need for doing just this, and they can fret and worry about it because that Virgo voice won't be stilled. That fretting can even make them ill in some cases.

Developing that Virgo side is extremely difficult for Librans because, like any twelfth house motivation or ability, it's most easily got to grips with by being alone with time to reflect and draw up that unconscious side. Yet Libra is often drawn to others to develop his creativity, as we've seen from the Leo rulership of the eleventh house. Since Leo is such a powerful influence, many Librans never will develop the Virgo side of themselves; they will stay reflectors of other people's brilliance rather than developing their own potential. But it may be that this is the easier thing for them to do – and Libra will usually do what is easiest for him!

☆ ☆ ☆

Libra is a generally happy, charming and likeable sign to be born under. Librans aren't strong, powerful people, but there are enough of them around anyway; Libra is tactful, graceful, diplomatic and wants to see an end to those problems the rest of us argue about all the time. With others, he can develop effective ways of dealing with them. This sounds a pretty good deal for the other eleven signs!

Scorpio rising
THE SCORPION

The symbol of the scorpion tells us quite a lot – but not everything – about the person with Scorpio rising. The scorpion has strong external 'armour', and of course it has that deadly sting. But perhaps the key thing is where it lives – in very inhospitable places and climates. The scorpion endures; and likewise the person with Scorpio rising has a tremendous power of being, a refusal ever to knuckle under or submit.

Scorpio is possessed of great energy and determination, and endless depths of willpower. The sheer force of Scorpio can be quite frightening. When Scorpio's mind is fixed on something – when Scorpio *needs* something (for Scorpio, any want or desire *is* a need; there are no half measures here) he can force his way to it, and possess it, or he'll die trying. The fixity and intensity of Scorpio's drives are unparalleled in the Zodiac. If you have enemies, pray that none of them are Scorpios.

But. . . Scorpio is not capable of tact or subtlety. Scorpio does not stop to analyse problems and figure out the best or easiest way of getting what he wants. He simply knows that his desires are so intense that he *will* get those things. And there is always something hidden, secret, about Scorpio. Scorpio can be a stranger to himself in extreme cases, and he prefers not to discuss himself too much with others.

Scorpio is also the most maligned sign in the Zodiac; he has an evil and sinister reputation which is undeserved. It's been fixed on him by people who cannot understand his depths of passion. But Scorpio's drive to transform things around him – which he feels, intuitively, his unequalled power of will can do – can work for good or evil. Gandhi was born with Scorpio rising, and it's clear in which direction his Scorpio energies worked.

Scorpio's general personality overlay is one of *passion and intensity*. There is never any laid-back or nonchalant quality about him.

SECOND HOUSE (MONEY)
Ruler Sagittarius

This is a mixed blessing. For Scorpio, the good news is that Sagittarius brings him luck with money. Scorpio may inherit money, win it in competitions, get unexpected pay rises, make fortunate investments – almost anything can turn up trumps out of the blue (this isn't saying that everything will work perfectly, of course).

On the other hand, Sagittarius loves extravagance. Scorpio is not averse to this under some circumstances either, so he needs to be careful with planning his finances. Scorpio is likely to earn a lot and spend a lot, so he may need to cultivate his selling techniques. Not too difficult; Sagittarius is inventive and the 'charming rascal' element of the Centaur-Archer, allied to Scorpio's drive, can produce the goods.

Scorpio may enjoy using money he earns to broaden his mind, maybe through buying books, but also through travelling to distant countries. Sagittarius wants to do this, and going to completely different places and cultures touches something within Scorpio, his desires for transforming and changing things. Such places give him insights into other people's lives which are very different from his own and this he appreciates. Money *as such* does not usually matter to Scorpio; it's the way that money gives him the ability to extend his powers he likes.

THIRD HOUSE (COMMUNICATING)
Ruler Capricorn

Now we can see why Scorpio has a reputation for being secretive. Capricorn is a careful and conservative influence, and Scorpio is generally given to concealing things about himself. Scorpio usually only communicates when he wants to, and he is very careful about what he says. Scorpio chooses words carefully, writes with attention to detail, and there is nothing superfluous. Scorpio says what he needs to and no more.

What's more, Scorpio is direct in his communicating and hardly puts things over with maximum charm. Capricorn isn't concerned with such things and Scorpio's sting can come over here. Scorpio can be harsh, hard-hearted and abrasive in the way he expresses himself. He is only interested in putting over what he needs, and he isn't very responsive to the nature of other's replies.

This dispassionate, almost dehumanized element in Scorpio can make him the perfect scientist (but not in social science). After all, science is built on the dehumanized, alienated idea that the observer (scientist) and the object of his scrutiny are quite separate things. The observed 'thing' doesn't affect the scientist in any way, and Scorpio is often just like this.

Scorpio is no charmer. Others have to be able to take his intensity and directness, or he washes his hands of them as soft-headed ninnies. But the Scorpio power is still there, and Capricorn's straight-to-the-point quality can make Scorpio a riveting speaker. It's just that you don't get to talk back much.

FOURTH HOUSE (HOME)
Ruler Aquarius

Scorpio's home will never be a conventional, run-of-the-mill place with this influence on the fourth house. Scorpio is likely to have a new house rather than an old one (whether renovated or not) and the design is likely to be odd. Scorpio will often suddenly get it into his head to change things by knocking down a wall to create one large room where there were two, installing a whole range of new technology from the TV–video complex to a microwave and dishwasher and new washing machine. Aquarius wants new things and it wants change and it wants it *now*. Adding Scorpio's intensity and refusal to compromise to this, life can be eventful.

Scorpio's domestic arrangements with his family may be unusual too. Scorpio may be away from home a lot (Aquarius gets restless and bored easily) and he may have an open marriage or a common law spouse (but Taurus' rulership of the seventh house will create problems here). His children are likely to be given an unusual education in some way (perhaps at a boarding school if Scorpio can afford it) and quite a lot of it may be given in the home. Scorpio can, if anything, be rather offhand about his children at times, more easy-going than one might expect, and even appear neglectful at times. But they are aware of the Scorpion's passionate love of them nonetheless.

Scorpio children need novelty and unusual ways of stimulating them and holding their attention when they are young. They are sentimental about their parents, fiercely proud of them, and love them deeply, but they do not readily show this. The intensity of their affections is too much for them to know how to handle. Wise parents of Scorpio children will understand this, and will avoid drawing this out of them. Scorpio needs his secrecy.

FIFTH HOUSE (CREATIVITY)
Ruler Pisces

This is tricky. Scorpio has one deep drive which affects his creativity more than any other: something in Scorpio wants desperately to be immortal, to be remembered after his death for what he has achieved. Whether Scorpio understands this is another matter, but it's true all the same. Pisces does not bring clear thinking or any natural ease of achievement to Scorpio; but Scorpio will not be denied. Nothing, not even the confusions of Pisces, can prevent Scorpio having what he truly desires. It just makes life more difficult. Scorpio finds that when he puts his unstinting efforts into some creative project or other – anything from decorating to writing the great 20th-century novel – it's almost impossible to think straight. All he can do is allow himself to be driven along by the force of his belief in himself and see how things work out. Many times they won't. When they do, that's enough. Scorpio forgets his failures fast.

The positive aspect of Pisces' influence is that it can bring Scorpio the streak of pure genius to create something breathtaking. Pisces, the dreamer, can imagine and conceive of things which others would not dare to; and Scorpio may be given to the study of unusual things such as mysticism or even poetry (sounds pretty unlikely for Scorpio, doesn't it? Well, Pisces is sentimental enough to make it possible). Pisces also gives Scorpio a love of seclusion when he is working in this way; he wants no-one else and, until he's finished, he has nothing he wishes to say anyway.

Pisces also brings an unexpected sentimentality to Scorpions in their romances. Scorpio is the most passionate lover imaginable; he almost seeks to exhaust himself utterly through sex and his possessiveness and jealousy are well known (and, for once, his reputation is deserved). But Scorpio idealizes his loved ones too and he is unrealistic about them. He seeks an impossible perfection and he is always, at heart, unsatisfied. His passions are so deep that they probably couldn't be satisfied anyway. He is prone to having some disastrous and even scandalous affairs; Scorpio's intense drives know no morality and Pisces hardly makes up for that. Partners of Scorpios have interesting lives.

SIXTH HOUSE (WORK/SERVICE)
Ruler Aries

One aspect of the sixth house is the way in which we are of service to others through work in the most general sense. For Scorpio, no way. Aries never served anyone. It's out of the question.

But, in work generally, Scorpio has unparalleled energy. He is intensely ambitious anyway (Leo's rulership of the tenth house) and the Aries energy added to Scorpio's drives – this combination couldn't possibly be equalled. Scorpio *devours* work. He seems to be able to do the work of five men, and he works round the clock whenever the feeling to do so takes him (which is a lot of the time). His stamina is prodigious. He can accomplish tasks so difficult that others wouldn't even bother to think about how they could be done.

Scorpio has one major problem here. He is dominating and bossy and he can be abrasive. Scorpio expects others to get what they want in life as he does; by unstinting effort and without asking help from others (Scorpio very rarely does this). Scorpio will only help those who help themselves, and he is not sensitive to the feelings of less robust or talented people than himself. Scorpio bosses may be respected by those who work for them but they are never loved and rarely liked. Scorpio *has* to develop a greater awareness of the problems of others at work. Not even his prodigious abilities can achieve all he wants alone. Scorpio should try such things as regular feedback sessions from those who work for him, keeping quiet at the time (not so hard for him) and spending at least some time thinking things over later. A good work partner or secretary can also be a godsend to him. Sagittarians are a good bet, since they are one of the very few signs which can both humour Scorpio and outwit him.

SEVENTH HOUSE (MARRIAGE/PARTNERSHIPS)
Ruler Taurus

Now life begins to get complicated again. The Aquarian influence on Scorpio's fourth house tends to make him attracted to unusual marriage arrangements but Taurus is very practical and very conservative. Scorpio's own drives are so strong that he is almost amoral about such matters. This is a difficult matter for him. Often, Scorpio may have one marriage followed by a later, less formal partnership arrangement. Something in Scorpio (the Taurus influence) wants a steady, secure marriage and Scorpio's intense desires can be rooted to that; but his jealousies, extremes of passion and the Aquarius influence making him like staying away from home now and then pull him in the opposite direction. This makes life hard for him and his partner, all the more so because Scorpio often can't put into words what is pulling him in different directions at the same time.

Matters are more straightforward where business partnerships are involved. Scorpios want to keep these very practical and tend to attract people of this type; they keep a careful eye on the finances and can be quite suspicious about them (both Scorpio and Taurus are prone to this). They are very correct in such dealings, rather cool and aloof, and they can actually be objects of suspicion themselves because of their secrecy. But Scorpios very rarely cheat; it's beneath them. Scorpios make excellent business partners and the combination of an industrious Scorpio with a rich backer (Taurus' affinity with wealth makes this a possibility – and don't forget that Sagittarius ruling the second house gives Scorpio the luck to get into this type of situation) is an ideal combination.

Something of the Taurus affinity with wealth and pleasure and beauty also rubs off on Scorpio's spouse; he will be generous in buying things for her which make her look grand and he takes great pride in this.

EIGHTH HOUSE (NEEDS FROM OTHERS)
Ruler Gemini

Gemini's influence gives Scorpio another advantage when it comes to expressing his material needs to others and getting their backing. He has natural luck, the ability to express himself concisely, he's a hard worker and is practical about partnerships. Now Gemini gives him the versatility to come up with good ideas for joint ventures. Some mix, this – clearly everything is leading up to the Leo factor of the tenth house, but more of that shortly.

Scorpio is naturally not very communicative but the Gemini influence gives him the ability to put over ideas cleverly and with some charm and great persuasiveness where his needs are concerned. He has the ability, and the drive, and he's going to use that combination. The practicality of his ideas adds to all this. Scorpio will not have problems getting backing for his ideas; maybe he creates for himself the luck which Sagittarius brings to his monetary affairs.

Gemini's influence tells us one last thing about Scorpio. Although he has everything going for him anyway, Scorpio knows that a lot of success in business and work depends on being in the right place at the right time and, above all, knowing the right people. Scorpio might not normally be sociable enough to manage all this but Gemini gives him the ability to do it, thus strengthening the one possible weakness in Scorpio as far as business and money affairs go.

NINTH HOUSE (FAR HORIZONS)
Ruler Cancer

Cancer's influence here gives the Scorpio person some unexpected features to his personality. In one way the influence is slightly negative – the Scorpio person's dreams, his religious beliefs, his philosophy of life, tend to be rather conditioned into him by his early family life and he can be constrained into over-conservative ways of thinking by that. But Cancer also gives Scorpio a compassion, a concern for others, which he might well otherwise lack.

Scorpio is distinctly emotional about ninth house affairs, and sensitive about them. He will not readily tolerate criticism of his views on religion, politics and the like and he is quick to take offence at it. He *may* be an altruist with fine ideals for humanity but he's often the kind of altruist who should keep away from direct contacts with other people!

Scorpio also has Cancer's moodiness and emotional restlessness when it comes to ninth house affairs. One specific effect of this is that Scorpio is often drawn to the sea, to voyages to places far away. Both Scorpio and Cancer are water signs and Cancer's restlessness and the ninth house need for travel and far horizons in the physical sense as well as the mental sense bring this about. Scorpio may travel to see distant relatives (the family connection of Cancer) or to learn about new places and people or both – the combination is ideal.

The prime lesson for Scorpio in ninth house affairs is this: the past often imprisons him. This is usually his family or his early education and conditioning. It is difficult to shed these influences – Cancer can be as tenacious as Scorpio – but unless they are shed Scorpio will not have a fulfilling vision of himself and his worth in life. Scorpio can transform himself and start anew; this will be painful given Cancer's influence but it needs to be done. Settling down or working in a different country from that of his birth, well away from family, can be an important liberating influence for a Scorpio.

TENTH HOUSE (CAREER)
Ruler Leo

This is where everything has been leading. Scorpio's strengths seem relentlessly to have been building up towards this: his communication skills, sound business partnership sense and his great capacity for work. And the Leo factor in Scorpio is ambition; he is driven to achieve great things. Scorpio is the dominator, the boss, the executive. Scorpio gets to the top because he holds most of the aces and his power and force is so great that he is hardly stoppable.

But when he makes it (there are unlikely to be any 'if's about this) he has earned it. Scorpio works for what he needs and he doesn't short-cut or swindle people. He will quite dispassionately step on people if he absolutely has to; he can be ruthless in that way; but Leo's pride does not permit Scorpio to cheat.

Scorpio *has* to get to the top, and he *has* to be admired for it (Leo again). These needs are as real to him as breathing is for anyone else. Scorpio is *driven* to this. Scorpio people have to realize that they absolutely cannot tolerate any job where there is no prospect of getting to the top. They will become unhappy and frustrated, and when the Scorpion's sting flashes people will get hurt. Scorpio can draw attention to himself (especially the attention of his temporary bosses – temporary because he'll be in their chair before too long) by his hard work and also by developing his ideas for money-making or money-saving projects of some kind. Demonstrations of initiative by Scorpio will almost always get the attention of the people who matter in his career.

Finally, Scorpio people need public images which are admired by others. The risk to this is from personal scandals (Leo's no stranger to dalliances and Scorpio's passions are intense) rather than from shady business involvements. This is an ever-present danger for many Scorpios, but some of them have the audacity and sheer charisma to be admired for their affairs too. But they shouldn't rely on it.

ELEVENTH HOUSE (FRIENDSHIPS)
Ruler Virgo

Another reason why Scorpio is careful with social contacts and doesn't give himself away too easily. Virgo's prudent, intellectual streak guides Scorpio carefully in his casual social contacts. He talks relatively little and what he says is carefully considered. In the pauses in conversation, and when others are talking, Scorpio is observing and analysing but what conclusions he comes to – well, he won't give them away easily. Scorpio is careful and rather critical about acquaintances. Soft-headed people, or people with any whiff of the overly unconventional or scandalous about them, are avoided very carefully.

Work and friendship are closely connected given the rulership of the eleventh house by Virgo, since this sign is associated with work and service. Scorpios meet a majority of social contacts through work (rather than through social or sports clubs or some other activity outside work) and they can be rather helpful to them. Scorpio's ambition does not prevent him from being genuinely helpful to social contacts – providing he thinks they're worth it. But then if they weren't, the Virgo influence would have weeded them out as undesirables anyway. The effect works both ways; Scorpio often gets practical assistance at work from relatively casual contacts, which can be anything from telling him about a new career opportunity to some new device they know of for storing, retrieving, filing this, that or the other.

Work friends are useful to Scorpio and he should cultivate them. It may be worth spending an extra half hour in the social club bar at work sometime rather than working all the overtime he can get or taking his work home every night (or both).

TWELFTH HOUSE (THE UNCONSCIOUS)
Ruler Libra

In one way, Libra's influence on Scorpio is his saving grace. Scorpio is possessed of incredible energies and no mean talents and he could be a nasty bit of work without this. The Libran influence filters through, though. Something in his unconscious guides Scorpio towards things which are good for others, which do promote harmony and understanding between people. Which is just as well; he's so ambitious that he could damage a lot of people otherwise. But usually he doesn't, unless the Libra influence is very weak.

Libra's influence is hidden in Scorpio and difficult for him to understand and come to terms with. He has enough trouble doing that with any part of himself, given the sheer force of his desires; for Scorpio to stop and think is very hard. Scorpio yearns sometimes for harmony, beauty, peace and rest from the depth of his emotions. The ideal place for him is in a secluded (twelfth house) beautiful (Libra) place; botanical gardens, a quiet art gallery, somewhere where he can be alone and let himself relax for once. Or it can just be at home, in a darkened room, listening to his favourite music. Libra's influence comes through emotionally to Scorpio, as all things must; he can feel peace and restfulness and he may also feel within himself something of the Libran need for fairness and justice in the world around him. Libra's laziness cannot subdue Scorpio's powerful drives; at these times, on his own, Scorpio can recharge his batteries and be inspired again by idealistic concerns. Scorpio needs this; just as he must have the chance to rise to the top at work he *must* spend time alone in beautiful places to keep in touch with a part of himself he knows is there but usually cannot understand.

But Libra's influence can point to one weakness in Scorpio which he must watch: an unconscious desire for self-indulgence and luxury. Scorpio may want that beautiful place where he can relax all the time, to buy it and keep it and luxuriate in it. That isn't the way it should work, and Scorpio must avoid this pitfall.

☆ ☆ ☆

Scorpio is one of the powerhouses of the Zodiac along with Aries. This sign is so intense and passionate that it almost sweeps all before it; you cannot ever stop a Scorpio but you can, fortunately, outwit him fairly easily. The trick lies in making very sure that he doesn't find out about it. Without Scorpio, other people's lives would probably be easier, at least emotionally, but they would also be improverished; a lot of work which needs doing would never get done. Scorpio can boss the rest of us about, but he earns the right to do so. Though we often don't love him for it – and he really doesn't deserve that – we ought to respect him.

Sagittarius rising
THE CENTAUR-ARCHER

The symbol for this sign flatters the Sagittarian, for it shows most of his virtues but none of his faults. The galloping centaur – the mythical half-man, half-horse – drawing his bow and firing his arrow to the heavens. The centaur is the fastest-moving sign in the Zodiac and this shows us Sagittarius' endless restlessness. Sagittarius never settles down, not really; and the mental facet of this is his absolutely unquenchable need for freedom, to do as he wishes, to come and go as he pleases. Nobody ever fitted a bit to a centaur. And his arrow: his ideas soar to the heavens, his words and gestures fly at us, almost overwhelming others. The sky to which his arrow flies shows the astrological element of Air, the thinking element, and although Sagittarius is a Fire sign, Sagittarius is an intellectual. He has to know, ponder, think, reflect, absorb every bit of knowledge he can.

Sagittarius also has some rather bad faults. He often lacks persistence; he starts a dozen things off at once and somehow never finishes any of them. He is tactless and not too patient with sensitive souls. He can take things, and people, for granted. But usually he manages to get away with this. Sagittarius is friendly, generous, enthusiastic, optimistic and almost always in a good mood. There is no-one better at cheering other people up when they're blue, and they forgive him a lot for that. Sagittarius' optimism inspires others; and he himself often has great and grand ideas. He is an idealist and is passionately concerned about social issues, religion, the way our society is organized and who has (and doesn't have) power and wealth in it. Sagittarius himself can be effective in doing things in these areas and he's always good at inspiring others to start *doing* something.

The general personality overlay of Sagittarius is the desire for knowledge and freedom, and his general optimism and good heart. A fortunate combination, and this sign is usually known as the lucky sign of the Zodiac. But it's not without its problems, and the second house shows us one immediately.

SECOND HOUSE (MONEY)
Ruler Capricorn

This is a potential conflict. The general Sagittarian personality is impulsive and generous and likes spending freely for himself and for his friends. But Capricorn is rather mean and extremely careful. The Capricorn influence wants to hoard money, Sagittarius wants to blow it in spending sprees. Sagittarians of both kinds can be found, depending on the strength of this Capricorn influence.

The solution for Sagittarius is this: he should budget carefully (Capricorn's influence means that Sagittarius can do this and he doesn't mind doing it too much) and put aside a regular sum each month for the bills. Add 10% for savings, then blow the rest. It can be helpful for Sagittarius to get help from others (Capricorn likes working with others to make money) like bank managers, accountants, friends or his spouse or partner to make sure he works out the regular budget sum right. Credit cards or anything similar which allow him impulse buying, Sagittarius should avoid like the plague.

Capricorn's influence can often mean, though, that even when Sagittarius blows his money it may go on purchases which are useful to him in some way. In fact, if the Capricorn influence is strong, Sagittarius may *only* spend money in this way and he may find it hard to handle luxury – a paradoxical quality a few Sagittarians do show. Capricorn may make Sagittarius fret and worry over money, too, another good reason for enlisting the help of others and taking those worries away. But at least it can give him the ability to get the rewards from his work that he deserves, often in middle-age rather than in his youth.

THIRD HOUSE (COMMUNICATING)
Ruler Aquarius

Sagittarius is a sociable creature anyway, and his mind works quickly; he is witty and entertaining. But the Aquarian influence gives him something more. Sagittarius with this influence can be ingenious, brilliant in his communicating; he can be captivating to listen to or a brilliant writer. Usually, in conversation, he will gesture freely and emphasize what he says strongly with body language and strong facial expressions. You *listen* to this man. Sagittarius can be both inventive and practical at the same time when getting his ideas across. Since this is what he most wants to do in life given the Leo influence on the ninth house, this is just as well.

The problem for Sagittarius comes from the impulsive, perverse side of Aquarius which reinforces one of his own faults. Aquarius, rebellious at times, can make Sagittarius say provocative things just for the hell of it. And Sagittarius can hurt; he can let fly verbal arrows which hit home and wound people. It is unusual for him to do this deliberately since he's rarely annoyed enough by others to do it (although when he is nobody can take another person to pieces verbally like an irate Sagittarian), but it just happens without conscious intent. Often Sagittarius can put down other people's ideas (just for playfulness in some cases) and hurt them badly by personalizing the exchange in the process ('Only a moron could believe *that*'). Ideas are so precious to Sagittarius that he defends them with everything he has (which is a formidable armoury), but he is not sensitive to how much other people may feel for their own ideas. Sagittarius wants to tell you about his ideas; he's right and you'd better believe it. He can certainly discuss things without being bigoted or unreasonable but in all truth the object of the exercise is to convert you to his way of looking at things. Sagittarius needs to develop greater sensitivity to how other people feel about their ideas, and to bite back sarcastic rejoinders every now and then – at least to start with.

FOURTH HOUSE (HOME)
Ruler Pisces

Sagittarius often likes his home to have a place within it where he can retreat. Sometimes he may not live in his own home at all; he may live in university lodgings, a rectory, accommodation owned by the people he works for, and so on. Sagittarius is not sure he really likes 'home' much (Pisces is not clear-headed and Sagittarius loves freedom), and he may avoid having one. But he still needs that place of retreat (the seclusive influence of Pisces). He will need to work, or more likely study and contemplate, within it. While he likes having friends around and being hospitable there must be times he can count on where he's got the place to himself. Hell, for Sagittarius, is living with other people when he doesn't care for them.

Likewise married Sagittarians or Sagittarians with partners tend to stay away from home a lot or like their partners to do the same. They may insist on having their own private room, which may puzzle or upset their partner (it doesn't seem that Sagittarius is too committed to this partnership) but it shouldn't when they understand his need to think in solitude. Generally, indeed, Sagittarius is not a house-trained creature. It may take a lot of time to persuade him to help much with housework, which he hates. The great mistake is to try and develop a rota for housework or some formal scheme for regular efforts. Sagittarius feels his freedom restricted and off he goes. He does more or less everything in sudden bursts of enthusiasm. He'll leave his house getting dirty and dusty for weeks and suddenly spend eighteen hours getting it spotless. It's just the way he is.

Sagittarian children are often affectionate to, and sentimental about, their parents and family homes but they're strongly independent and quite capable of leaving it all behind in adolescence. Wise parents make sure they allow young Sagittarians plenty of rope (never, *ever*, tell a Sagittarian he *must* be home by some particular time but nonchalantly comment when he has come home at four in the morning that a phone call home to tell his parents he'll be out late would be appreciated). That will avoid later breaks and tears – mostly from the parents, not the Sagittarian. Sagittarian parents are often better news for their children than Sagittarian children are for their parents, since they are kindly, generous and rather proud of their offspring. They also make strong efforts to educate them and stimulate their minds when young, but may become alienated from them if they turn out not to be as intelligent as they'd hoped. Some Sagittarian parents may need to realize that those children still need their love as much as the brighter ones in the family.

FIFTH HOUSE (CREATIVITY)
Ruler Aries

A powerful influence this: the strong energy and drive of Aries influences Sagittarius' creativity. Sagittarius is hardly short of ideas at any time, and Aries spurs him on to greater efforts. Fortunately, Aries also gives Sagittarius greater persistence than he might otherwise have, and when it comes to developing ideas in practical form, the Aries influence helps. Sagittarius may often work in bursts; add Sagittarian impulsivity and restlessness to Aries energy and what you get is a person who will rouse himself periodically and throw himself into creative effort (anything from decorating to writing) for a long stretch. At such times he can even outdo a Scorpio for sheer effort. At such times he may hardly sleep for a few days until he exhausts himself. It may not be the best way to work, but it may be the easiest for Sagittarius. For this reason, such things as flexible hours working and self-employment may be a good idea for him.

Sagittarians are also aggressive and energetic in romance. Sagittarius is rather inclined to fantasies and a bit unrealistic about such things; the Centaur would like to be a knight in white armour (a version of this can apply to female Sagittarians too). But Aries makes him passionate and he is drawn to dynamic and even aggressively sexy people; he is a very physical person and quite demanding. He is also restless and rather unfaithful. In this, he's as bad as Leo if not worse; Sagittarius is so curious, so fond of new people, that he is always looking at the pretty girl walking down the street. Mind you, he wants to talk to her too! Sagittarius can often divorce the physical side of things from his affections (the Centaur is half-man, half-animal) and he may genuinely feel that occasional casual sex isn't, really, being unfaithful to his partner. Potential partners of Sagittarians had better be aware of this and also that Sagittarius is not going to change. And, of course, above everything else he has to feel free in his relationships.

SIXTH HOUSE (WORK/SERVICE)
Ruler Taurus

Taurus gives the Sagittarian the ability to be very practical at work, and it gives him some extra persistence too. Sagittarius hankers after work which is slightly artistic or at least wants to work in pleasant surroundings, but perhaps the strongest effect of Taurus' influence is to make Sagittarius want to be paid fairly for his work. Despite his idealism and enthusiasm, Sagittarius won't work too hard if he can't see a clear material gain. This doesn't have to be an immediate prospect – Sagittarius is fairly far-sighted – but there must be a very definite possibility.

Sagittarius can be slightly self-indulgent about his work, and it can be fairly easy for him to say 'Oh, to hell with this' and laze about for a while. Taurus doesn't mind that. But since Sagittarius tends to work in intense bursts anyway, this may not be a fatal flaw. Taurus' influence also suggests that Sagittarians need others to help them with developing the practical side of their work – in particular, if they can , it's a good idea to delegate the details of work projects to others who enjoy looking after such things (Virgos are the ideal candidates. Virgos also tend to respect Sagittarians as having minds worth exchanging ideas with).

Health-wise, Sagittarians are robust given the Taurus influence, but the problem is over-indulgence, especially with sticky, sweet and rich foods. Sagittarians are sometimes overweight, and rather than dieting it is best for them to take exercise (Sagittarians do usually like sports) to burn off the excess calories.

SEVENTH HOUSE (MARRIAGE/PARTNERSHIPS)
Ruler Gemini

Sagittarians are attracted to physical, sexy people but they also want someone who is witty, versatile, and intelligent – in short, someone who has Gemini qualities. Rather demanding creatures, Sagittarians. But they do usually succeed in attracting people with Gemini qualities, and those people often are of help to them in practical ways, in developing their ideas or at work or at home.

The Gemini quality adds to Sagittarius' tendencies to unfaithfulness. Gemini is every bit as restless and curious as Sagittarius and there are often several marriages (or at least two), many affairs and much curiosity about potential lovers. And the coolness of Gemini tends to make Sagittarius something of a loner, really, especially given that he's a freedom lover to start with; despite his passionate nature and enthusiasms, Sagittarius is *the* loner of the Zodiac. Certainly, he is loved more often than he loves others.

Sagittarius has the knack of getting together with people in business who can develop his ideas, make them tick, and often put them over to others. Gemini is the expert public relations man and although Sagittarius is no shrinking violet he may often prefer to leave it to such a partner to do the selling and put the message across to the public at large (and potential purchasers of whatever he's selling in particular). Sagittarius prefers coming up with the ideas to selling himself and his products.

Sagittarians *have* to work at jobs where they use their mental abilities to the full; Gemini's influence ensures that. Anything else is a waste of time, and will make Sagittarians irritable and depressed. Then verbal arrows will start flying.

EIGHTH-HOUSE (NEEDS FROM OTHERS)
Ruler Cancer

Sagittarians are not forthcoming about their needs given this influence. They may also use a subtle form of emotional blackmail on people; there's a promise of withdrawal from others (Cancer's defensive reaction) if their needs are not met. They are also moody and rather capricious about things; they may enthusiastically request something one day and *appear* unconcerned (although they aren't) the next. Cancer's influence does not make it easy for Sagittarius to express his needs to others, nor for others to meet those needs given the emotional nature of his reactions to what they say. It's so out of character for him.

Given this Cancer influence it may be easiest for Sagittarius to get his needs across to others from his home base – writing from there, using the phone, meeting his friends for dinner parties and the like. He may feel more secure in this setting and Sagittarians who do have problems with expressing their material needs to others should try this tactic.

Sagittarius also has difficulty in expressing his emotional needs, given the Cancer rulership of the eighth house, which is usually more concerned with the material side of things. It seems odd that this gregarious, talkative person should have such problems but he often does. An inner insecurity may prevent him being forthcoming; this unexpected quality is often understood by close partners and friends who know him well.

NINTH HOUSE (FAR HORIZONS)
Ruler Leo

Like his astrological brother Gemini, Sagittarius is a 'perfect' sign; Leo, the emotional heart of him, rules the ninth house, and Sagittarius is the ninth sign in the Zodiac. Of course Sagittarius desires freedom above everything else: love, fame, money – these things mean nothing to him without freedom. Leo's rulership brings an intense yearning to Sagittarius to travel far and wide, both in the real world and in the realms of his imagination, learning all he can and growing as a person by doing it.

Likewise, Sagittarians are passionately interested in society, religion, and philosophy – their lives are living these things out. A Sagittarian *is* his ideas. Leo's regal quality, with Sagittarius' extrovert quality, together compel the Sagittarian to express these ideas to everyone who will listen (and he will only come and get you if you don't) with all the force of his being. Sagittarius is inspirational and he believes his ideas to be right (though, unlike Scorpions, you can at least argue the toss with Sagittarians). He has hundreds of ideas for improving society, the ways in which people live together, the running of schools and other educational institutions, law reform and just about everything else. His mind is inexhaustible. But, if you know an Sagittarians or if you are one yourself, you know these things all too well.

Whatever he does in *any* field of life Sagittarius *must* feel free. Leo's pride influencing this ninth house of dreams and imagination produces someone who cannot bear to be repressed in any way. Sagittarius *will* be free to think, say and write what he pleases when he pleases. This sign, given its urge to express these ideas, is very much the teacher of the Zodiac, and his deep concern for the freedom of the individual is a good first lesson.

TENTH HOUSE (CAREER)
Ruler Virgo

Just as Taurus ruling the sixth house gave Sagittarius the ability to be practical about his work, Virgo's rulership of the tenth makes him careful and prudent about what he chooses to do. Sagittarians are fairly calculating about their careers and they think about them, and the people involved with them, at some length. Indeed, they can often seem rather cool and aloof at work; Virgo is a critical and rather cool sign and this can influence Sagittarius. However, with work colleagues he knows fairly well, his natural extrovert personality will tend to come through readily enough.

Sagittarius can be very critical, though, with others at work. For one thing, Sagittarius is tactless and lets those arrows fly off anyway, but add Virgo's critical qualities to this and you have someone who can be quite devastating in putting other people down if they seem a little dumb or slow on the uptake. This may often be an off-the-cuff impulse with Sagittarius, and even if it's only resorting to the old remedy of counting to ten before saying anything when he's irritated by someone at work, he needs to find a way of avoiding this.

Virgo's influence again stresses how Sagittarians must use their minds at work – there must be problems to solve and Sagittarius is really very good at this. He's imaginative enough, Virgo gives him practicality and an eye for detail, and he can express his ideas and solutions to others without much trouble. A happy mix.

Sagittarians also like to appear well-organized at work and are fussy about their work, and public, reputations. They are sarcastic and really quite verbally vicious to anyone questioning them about such things.

ELEVENTH HOUSE (FRIENDSHIPS)
Ruler Libra

Well, this is why Sagittarians get away with it. Other people forgive them their faux pas and occasional sarcasms because they're rather charming friends. It is not possible to remain angry with a Sagittarian for long, if only because they have such charming manners and clearly never get angry with friends for any length of time themselves. Sagittarians disarm you by being charming, friendly and, of course, interesting to talk to. They always have ideas to discuss with you and, with the Libra influence, they *love* to talk with friends and they express themselves gracefully and well.

Sagittarians like agreeable company and they will usually avoid people they don't care for (there's something of Libra's avoidance of problems in this). They *do* like friends they can rely on; undependable people will be cut quietly out of their social circles (of which they have many). Likewise, they are drawn to artistic, beautiful, even-tempered friends (ones with Libran qualities) and, given Libra's association (as the seventh sign) with the seventh house of marriage and partnerships, they may well marry a friend they've known for some time when they do marry – if they ever do. And, if they do, for one or other of their marriages.

TWELFTH HOUSE (THE UNCONSCIOUS)
Ruler Scorpio

The rulership of the twelfth house, of secret and hidden things, by this powerful sign – no stranger to secrecy, Scorpio – gives Sagittarians great power and resources. Deep within them is an intense drive to endure, a desire to project power within them through the ideas they express. Scorpio can also give Sagittarians a magnetic, charismatic quality which can almost bewitch those who listen to them. Behind the ideas lives an almost elemental force, willing others to submit and agree with them. This is a powerful placement for Scorpio and the hidden resourcefulness and willpower it gives Sagittarius are strong assets for him.

The negative side is twofold. Scorpio's influence can make Sagittarius a fanatic; his inner convictions are so intense he will brook no argument or discussion. Also, Sagittarius can bring about his own downfall through Scorpio's weaknesses – not least disastrous sexual affairs or intense secrecy which makes others suspicious of him.

Sagittarius needs to come to terms with the Scorpio power in him when he is alone, as with all twelfth house affairs. Through quiet thought, meditation exercises and the like, he can realize this great potential within him and ask himself what he's going to do with it. Sagittarius is not short of ideas on this point and if Scorpio's energies are harnessed to the altruistic, humanitarian streak in Sagittarius then a powerfully good person is at work in the world.

☆ ☆ ☆

Sagittarius is a lucky and happy-tempered sign to be born under. Enchanted by ideas and his mulling over them, the Sagittarian is endlessly persuading the rest of us that if only what he suggested was acted on them all would be well . . . well, maybe. But Sagittarius forces us to think and he is a great teacher. And while he'd love us to agree with him his respect for individual freedom is so great he probably would fight tooth and nail for our right to say the opposite of what he believes to be true. This alone makes it worth putting up with his faults. Remember that, the next time you wince as one of the Archer's verbal barbs hits you.

Capricorn rising
THE GOAT

The mountain goat is a tenacious animal. It extracts a living (if you like) from an inhospitable and poor world and it's as tough as nails. Just so Capricorn; discipline, hard work, making a lot from little and patience are the hallmarks of this sign. Capricorn is a slow person but what he builds endures. And Capricorn has no time for frippery; Capricorn is serious, even rather melancholy and blue, with no sense of humour, so it seems.

Well, this is not entirely true. Capricorns don't like self-indulgence much and Scrooge probably was a Capricorn. And they aren't very forthcoming, either. But the mountain goat has a reputation, to put it bluntly, of being a rather randy animal, and Capricorn has his pleasures too. Life is not all bowls of gruel for Capricorn. The point is that he has his priorities, and he does want security and wealth before he can feel relaxed and enjoy himself. If Capricorn goes out for a meal, he will be sure that he can spare enough money for the meal (twice over), the taxi trips there and back (adding 50% to the most pessimistic estimate of the fare), and a spare £20 just in case. Capricorn is very practical about his pleasures. But he does have pleasures in life!

The general personality overlay of Capricorn is all about *patience* and a need for material security. These general aspects of personality affect virtually all areas of Capricorn's life.

SECOND HOUSE (MONEY)
Ruler Aquarius

There's a good side, and a bad side, here. To start with, Capricorn wants money – we all do, but Capricorn *longs* for money. Capricorn is a builder and a developer and he wants money – but, in honesty, not just for what he can do with it but because it's security for him. And Aquarius brings two fortunate influences. First, Capricorns have the ability to work in groups to obtain money, with others. Although Capricorn is rather quiet and keeps his personal affairs to himself, he's quite happy to do this, and Aquarius is a gregarious influence. And, most of all, Aquarius makes Capricorn really ingenious with money. Capricorn almost seems to be able to create the stuff out of thin air at times. He may be a brilliant speculator and whoever devised the phrase 'creative accounting' must have been a Capricorn! With Capricorn's practicality and Aquarius' originality, Capricorns have everything going for them so far as earning money goes. They see opportunities and they work ceaselessly to make something of them, no matter how small.

The negative side is quite unexpected. A little voice within Capricorn (the Aquarius influence) urges him to spend some, impulsively, from time to time. Aquarius is rebellious and stubborn and it wants to spend money for the hell of it every so often. Poor Capricorn! This makes him very unhappy and rather nervous. It's the last thing he really wants to do yet he really does seems to have these perverse inclinations sometimes, which he doesn't understand.

There is a way round this. Capricorn is a brilliant budgeter and he can work out how much he *could* spare for a little self-indulgent impulse spending now and then. When the mood comes, he can do just this; and small-scale investments in unlikely and improbable ventures might even come to something. The Aquarius influence can then murmur 'I told you so' to him and he can spare a little more next time.

THIRD HOUSE (COMMUNICATING)
Ruler Pisces

Of course Capricorn is rather introvert and keeps to himself with this sign ruling the third house! Outside things he knows very well, Capricorn is not at all sure of himself. He is rather shy, and very sensitive to what others will think of him. He feels a sense of inferiority about his ideas and his ability to express himself clearly and he dreads being put down because he is talking about something he doesn't know so much about (even when only opinions are involved, not facts). Capricorn may well avoid the company of other people for this very reason.

But when he is on sure ground – well, that can be different. Pisces can give him inspiration. Intuitively Capricorn *knows* the heart of the problem and his very practical mind can work out the details of the solution. Then he can put it across to others, in ways which are sensitive to their likely reactions (Pisces' influence again). Capricorn will do a lot of puzzle-solving alone given this Pisces influence; he may work in groups but he will retreat off somewhere when there's some real tough sorting-out to be done on the problem front.

Capricorn may not realize that Pisces' influence makes him a sensitive communicator with others and that other people may sense this and like him for it, even if he can't always express himself as he'd like to. Friends of Capricorns should understand Capricorn's sense of inferiority and show him that they value his sensitive, empathic qualities. It may well surprise him and draw him out of himself more.

FOURTH HOUSE (HOME)
Ruler Aries

Capricorn is aggressively proud of his home and puts a lot of energy into it. His reputation as a builder of things surely has something to do with Aries' energies ruling the fourth house – some Capricorns have been known *literally* to build their own homes. Never suggest that Capricorn's home isn't all it might be (for whatever reason). Capricorn can have a fearful temper on that score.

Aries' influence here is really not too good. Capricorn's families frequently have screaming arguments and there is often a lot of discord in the home. Capricorn himself may develop an emotional coldness and aloofness to protect himself from the pain of family conflicts – this seems to be a not uncommon thing for Capricorn children. This sign is not often a happy one in early life. Likewise, Capricorn parents may be too cold to love their children enough, thinking that looking after their material well-being is sufficient, that this is their duty (duty is a powerful concept for Capricorns). Capricorns may also couple this emotional coldness with a harsh dominance of their families which creates hidden frustrations and anger.

There's a Catch-22 about solving these problems: Capricorns who are aware of them will probably have tried to deal with them and those who aren't won't try anyway, in all likelihood. Given Aries' association with physical energies, sports, tough physical activities and the like can be a way of harmonizing the family; Capricorn parents who can play sports with their children may have a natural outlet for this aggression and it can even help strengthen bonds between them. This may sound like a variant of the cross-country running as therapy for libido principle so beloved of English public schools but it may actually work for Capricorns.

FIFTH HOUSE (CREATIVITY)
Ruler Taurus

Capricorn as the builder again. Capricorn is practical and conservative in what he dreams up and creates. Although Aquarius ruling the second house gives him a spark of genius with money, most of the time Capricorn treads along well-mapped roads with his creations. He will find slightly different uses for well-tried and tested things, or slightly more efficient ways of doing things, rather than coming up with anything really new. But Capricorn is very reliable: given a problem he'll come up with something to help out when the creative genius down the corridor is still agonizing over revolutionizing the whole business. Taurus is steadfast and reliable. So is Capricorn, and the influences come together. Cutting corners well, saving one or two percent here and there – that's what Capricorn excels at. Multiply that throughout a whole system, at work or at home, and Capricorn can save himself or others a small fortune.

In romance, the goat's reputation must have something to do with the strength and earthy quality of the bull. Capricorn is rather practical about courtship and, yes, I'm afraid he probably *is* counting the pennies and whether the object of his affections is rich or not *is* relevant to him, but he's not without virtues. Capricorn is a surprisingly sensuous animal and he does have an intuitive sense of gracefulness and beauty. He may not be as extravagant as others but a tasteless extravagance is not to be preferred to a simple but lovely gift of some kind. And Capricorn is faithful and devoted. When he has chosen his mate he has chosen for life, as the seventh house will also show us.

And finally, Capricorn *can* indulge himself. Taurus is a bit on the greedy side and a bit of luxury won't go amiss. Having checked that he can afford it, Capricorn will cheerfully take you out to dinner and you certainly won't be hungry afterwards.

SIXTH HOUSE (WORK/SERVICE)
Ruler Gemini

Another helpful influence on Capricorn's work ability. Gemini's rulership of the sixth house makes Capricorn versatile and intelligent with his work; he is able to pinpoint problems, think them through, and come up with detailed, practical solutions. He can also think surprisingly fast about matters of fine detail at work, although he may prefer to do this on his own (the Pisces influence on the third house).

Capricorn can also handle several jobs at once, and a change is as good as a rest for him. He may well have his work meticulously organized, so that he does job A in the morning, job B after lunch and before afternoon tea and job C to finish off with. This type of work schedule, with some variety in it, is ideal for Capricorn.

Capricorn can be a good work manager given the Gemini influence, because it makes it easy for him to talk to others about work and his ideas, and he enjoys socializing with people from work. His advice is practical and he is helpful to others; this makes them grateful to him and, coupled with his honesty and hard work, his work mates think well of him.

If there's one major thing Capricorn has going for him at work it's his efficiency; Gemini brings him this virtue. Capricorns don't waste time and they know how to organize themselves and others to get the best results at work.

SEVENTH HOUSE (MARRIAGE/PARTNERSHIPS)
Ruler Cancer

Capricorns are devoted to their partners in marriage and they want to marry only once; their loved one will be with them for life. They are very emotional about them, easily hurt, and rather sensitive. There is often an inbalance somewhere in a Capricorn's marriage. Either Capricorn depends too much on his partner emotionally or the reverse is true, depending on whether the Cancer influence most affects Capricorn himself or his choice of mate. And, as we've seen,

Aries ruling the fifth house can make Capricorn's home a bit of a battleground. Capricorn does not find domestic happiness easily, and yet Cancer's influence makes him long for just this. He may often feel insecure in his marriage.

Capricorn treats his closest friends as if they were members of the family, and he is again very sensitive to their feelings about him. He treats them well, and has a deep and genuine concern for their happiness. It is not easy to befriend a Capricorn, since they tend to shyness, but as close friends they are loving and loyal. They often have a maternal, protective attitude to their friends.

Since business partnerships are important anyway for Capricorn – he likes working with others, provided they give him the time and space to do some of that work alone – it's not surprising that Cancer can make him feel quite emotional about business partners too. Capricorn likes to watch over such partners and protect them, and he forms strong personal attachments to them.

EIGHTH HOUSE (NEEDS FROM OTHERS)
Ruler Leo

How the Leo factor works in people with Capricorn rising is a complex matter. To start with, Leo's power and self-assurance gives Capricorn the ability to project his needs (material needs rather then emotional ones) well. Capricorn needs funds and he can get them; he can build from the help he is given by others. But Leo's powerful influence makes this more personal. When Capricorn expresses a material need he is expressing *himself*. If he gets his needs met, if he gets money and backing and support, he can build more wealth and in doing that he feels a better person, stronger within himself. Capricorn's sense of self-worth is directly linked to how well he is able to build on help received form others. Understanding this, we can see why Capricorn has to have money and security and why he has a reputation as a builder of things which endure. Only in this way does he feel that he can endure himself. So Capricorn's love of wealth is not greed or selfishness but an absolute *need* within him, given this Leo influence. Capricorn must have deposit accounts, stocks and shares or just a post office savings account because he is isn't just saving money, he's stabilizing his own mind and personality by doing that. The way to Capricorn's heart is indeed via his cheque book, but matters are not as simple or as cold-hearted as that suggests.

Likewise Capricorn must have control over money in any dealings with others – in domestic finance at home, in business, in any sphere of activity. Since Capricorns are very responsible with money this is rarely a bad arrangement for the other partner(s).

NINTH HOUSE (FAR HORIZONS)
Ruler Virgo

Non-nonsense people, Capricorns, and Virgo's rulership here still further supports Capricorn's practicality (just as Taurus ruling the fifth house did). Capricorn is not really a dreamer or inventive genius. His view of life is based on efficiency, logic and common sense (what *he* sees as common sense, that is).

Obviously there's a good side to this. When Capricorn has ideas for changing things at work, or in the law or society generally, they are ideas which can at least work. Socialist Utopias built on pipe-dreams are not going to get much change from Capricorn (he tends to be conservative with a small 'c'). Capricorn has the ability to force himself and others to come up with consistent and logical ideas. Capricorns must make the best drafters of new legislation in the Zodiac. Without them, inspired ideas would come to little.

The negative side is fairly obvious, but with the critical quality of Virgo it can be very dampening for others: Capricorn demands that ideas should be practical from the word go. Capricorn doesn't readily understand that it can be important for more inspired (but less realistic) people simply to throw ideas around, to spark off new insights from each other, without being hassled by Capricorn saying 'Yes, but will it work?' every two minutes. Capricorn needs to be able to leave such people to their own devices, saying to himself that indeed they're probably a bunch of soft-headed wets but they just *might* come up with something he can turn into something useful eventually. It's probably better for him to be out of the way when they are throwing ideas around (he won't be able to stop criticizing them if he's there) and so Capricorn should know when to withdraw from brainstorming sessions.

TENTH HOUSE (CAREER)
Ruler Libra

Of course Capricorn likes to work with others to build things together. How could he not, with Libra's socializing influence affecting this house? Capricorn delights in working with others to put his ideas into practice. Certainly he needs time alone to work his ideas out, but when he has the basics straight, talking with others to sort out the fine detail and getting things moving please him greatly.

Libra also makes Capricorn friendly to workmates and it gives him a strong sense of justice and fair play at work. He is absolutely scrupulous at work and will not see people treated badly or any underhand activity going on. With these skills, any role as an executive, bargainer, conciliation service worker or trade union official is perfect for Capricorn. He will be admired by others for the fair-mindedness he brings to solving industrial problems.

Capricorn also has the ability to gain the respect and favours of those who are in superior positions at work. They see his hard-working nature, honesty and fairness and tend to respond well to him. This is often the way in which Capricorn makes progress in his career and Capricorns should try to catch the boss's eye by being in the right place at the right time (but *not* by talking too much or too loudly when he's around).

ELEVENTh HOUSE (FRIENDSHIPS)
Ruler Scorpio

Scorpio's strong energies work in intriguing ways for Capricorn. For one thing, Capricorn likes the casual friendship of strong, dynamic people; he likes people with the qualities of the Scorpion. There are very few weak or ineffectual people in Capricorn's social circles; he wants to see evidence of drive, talent and commitment from them.

Secondly, Scorpio's influence shows us that Capricorn often develops his own power and motivations from circles of friends who stimulate him and challenge him. The Scorpio side of him comes out in his friendships. Often, though, Capricorn may like those friends to handle the more telling or difficult aspects of problems, they're working on; Capricorn may look after the details but his friends may supply the final burst of energy, the push to turn something useful into something really effective, a best-seller. This applies most at work, of course – but then Capricorn meets friends most readily at work anyway.

There may also be something secretive about Capricorn when it comes to friendships; Capricorn may use the services of others to do unexpected or difficult things out of the public eye or without his close associates even knowing. Capricorn may prefer different circles of friends to remain separate so that those who know him in one circle don't get the chance to compare notes with others from different social circles. There's nothing dishonest or peculiar about this; it's just the way Capricorn likes it. His friends shouldn't feel belittled or undervalued on that score.

TWELFTH HOUSE (THE UNCONSCIOUS)
Ruler Sagittarius

And, finally, this is why Capricorns so often seem serious, weighed down by the problems of life. They do not find it easy to develop the happy-go-lucky, optimistic Sagittarius side of themselves; this part of them is hidden, buried in the unconscious. The other problem the hidden Sagittarian qualities bring to Capricorn is a failure of nerve, sometimes, when any really grand project comes along. Sagittarius, expansive and optimistic, would grab the chance with both hands and work like a demon to get things done and make the idea work out; Capricorn lets it go and settles for something smaller but more certain of success.

These faults Capricorn has to resolve by himself. When he's alone, he can get in touch with his inner high spirits. Capricorn may often feel happiest alone, another reason why he's rather retiring. At peace with himself, he begins to feels that really things aren't so bad after all, that the pressure on him may not be so endless and he can let himself relax for a time. What's more, from time to time Capricorn may have feelings of futility about his life. What he does is stolid, secure, lasting and practical. But inside him there is that streak of inventiveness, a little touch of audacious thought and imagination, and it just might spark something off when he's alone without too much on his mind (this is especially true as he gets older). Capricorn needs to learn for himself in what environments this feeling comes over him, and cultivate that; this side of him badly needs developing by middle age or else he can become a colourless, unhappy and repressed person.

☆ ☆ ☆

There are certainly high-spirited and happier signs than Capricorn to be born under. But Capricorn has great virtues. His honest labouring, his fairness, his kindness to his friends and those he works with – Capricorn may not make the rest of us fall about laughing with his witty conversation but when things are bad and our lives chaotic there is no better or truer friend than the goat. And while the lighter side of him is often buried, it is still there. Anyone lacking at least one Capricorn friend is certainly missing something in life.

Aquarius rising
THE WATER-CARRIER

The symbol for this brilliant and characterful sign needs some explaining. The water-carrier is often shown as an angel, pouring out water freely. Although Aquarius is an Air sign, in this old symbol Water is representing intuition, insight, and Aquarius pours it over everyone he sees. And so Aquarius is potentially a genius, original, creative, unreliable but capable of moments of brilliant inspiration. And they are fiercely independent; apart from Sagittarians, no others need freedom as much as Aquarians.

Aquarians have some unfortunate weaknesses to balance these merits. Hand in hand with their independence goes a perverse stubbornness; Aquarians can say outrageous things and shock others just for the hell of it. They can be rebellious to the point of sheer crankiness. Neither are they overflowing with the milk of human kindness. Aquarians lack emotional depth and they are cool in their affections. This is very strongly a mental sign. They prefer casual friendships to deep attachments. They can sometimes be impractical, or even fanatical.

Summing up Aquarians is impossible, really: this is the most unpredictable sign in the Zodiac. Aquarius is capable of almost anything and there are always exceptions to the rules. In fact, Aquarius' general personality overlay is that of unpredictability and restlessness, and a very 'mental' approach to life. Life is never dull with these people around.

SECOND HOUSE (MONEY)
Ruler Pisces

This is unfortunate. Aquarians can be a disaster so far as financial planning goes. They simply have no idea of how to budget and they spend freely on impractical things. An Aquarian will cheerfully trot down to the local agitprop bookstore, spend his money and find he has nothing to eat for a week. Aquarius *could* put his mind to keeping a budget record and straightening his finances out – he has the ability – but he's always prone to impulse spending. There is *no* way he'll avoid that. Aquarius will *have* to enlist the help of others with his finances. It's either that or bankruptcy.

But Aquarius can get some financial luck. He is generous to a fault; Pisces makes him want to treat his friends well and delight them. And this doesn't go unnoticed by others, who tend to treat him well in return. Aquarius may attract lucky windfalls from others. He just has to find a way of not letting them evaporate.

At least Pisces softens Aquarius in this matter; Aquarius doesn't actually give a fig for money. He likes beautiful and strange, original, unusual things which he can buy with money, but he is never greedy and he is kinder to other people with his money than most.

Another important lesson for Aquarius, so far as making money goes, is that he may often isolate a need others have – a gap in the market, if you like – intuitively, given Pisces' influence. The odds are he will never get it together to exploit it, and he has to have a details man to work with him to put the idea into practical form. Since Aquarians like partnerships, this should work out well; Virgo, Capricorn and above all Gemini people are Aquarius' ideal partners here.

THIRD HOUSE (COMMUNICATING)
Ruler Aries

Now this person really wants to collar you and get his ideas inside your head! Aries makes Aquarius aggressive about his ideas. He is, it need hardly be said, never short of them. Aquarius can go out to the world and project his ideas with such force that people are simply overwhelmed by him. Aquarius' inventiveness coupled with the Aries fire can even create new modes of communicating; when the holographic equivalents of telephones come along Aquarius will have invented them.

The negative side is fairly obvious and Aquarius really has to watch for it. How much does Aquarius really *communicate*? Communication is a two-way process and although Aquarius loves playing ideas around the Aries influence can make him bullying and too certain of himself. He bulldozes others into submission and doesn't listen to them. He creates tension in conversations by his excessive aggression. If he's in a perverse or difficult mood this can be very unpleasant for everyone concerned. Aquarius *must* watch out for when he's in this kind of mood and avoid company at such times; there are other things he can do. The silent counting-to-ten and keeping your mouth shut trick will not work with him; he's too impetuous for this. So, if Aquarius can't keep quiet he must learn when to keep out of circulation, or know which friends can take his extremes and not bother about it (Sagittarians are the best bet).

FOURTH HOUSE (HOME)
Ruler Taurus

Aquarians may not generally be too bothered about money but they do hanker after lovely, expansive homes. This is where they want a little luxury in their lives. Often they will seek to create music, or decorate with art or even sculpture, at home. Taurus likes the artistic and so does Aquarius. There may be an odd blend of the traditional and the art nouveau, given Taurus' traditionalism and Aquarius' love of new and odd things. Such inconsistencies are no problem for Aquarius. Aquarius is a thinker and likes things worked out properly, but he's quite happy with paradoxes and contradictions, and his home can be like that. The oak dining table may be surrounded by gleaming creations in chrome steel and plastic.

Aquarius' family life is also an odd mix sometimes. Aquarians can be rather conservative about family life and certainly take care of their families financially. But their impulsiveness, and this clash between Taurus' conservative nature and Aquarius' progressive, rebellious instincts can create problems. Although Aquarius wants harmony at home he can be an awkward customer in the wrong moods. Again, it's a question of Aquarius knowing when to keep out of the way.

Aquarian parents, while providing for their children well, may not understand how children like predictability and security so far as their parents are concerned, any may be disappointed if the children aren't intellectually bright enough. Aquarian children are quite a handful for their parents, because they're moody and rebellious. They have to be given their heads and if allowed their own room with minimal interference and at least one night a week when they can do what they like (more or less) all will go reasonably well. But when the child is in an awkward mood no punishments will alter this; Aquarian children are stubborn little beasts and will *never* be bullied into admitting that they were wrong in some misdeed. Given freedom and their own time, they'll do this of their own accord.

FIFTH HOUSE (CREATIVITY)
Ruler Gemini

Aquarius is a fertile creature when it comes to ideas. He has the Aries energy to project them and now Gemini makes him an endless source of ingenious ideas. Gemini also makes him rather more practical than he might be otherwise, especially if he works developing these ideas with other people (the effect of Gemini's influence, and Aquarius is sociable anyway).

Since Aquarius is an Air sign, and Gemini strongly intellectually inclined, Aquarius is an ideas man at an almost exclusively mental level. There is a lack of emotion, or passion, about the things he creates (although he projects ideas with real aggression). Aquarius tends to be concerned more with things than with people. He is an inventor, a creator of new *things*. He is also a fine critic, given the ability Gemini has in this area; Aquarius is good at analysing his own creations to see if they work or not.

In romance, Aquarius is definitely cool. Gemini's influence makes sure of this. What turns Aquarius on is mental stimulation; he is attracted to fast-thinking, amusing, highly intelligent people. He is, of course, completely unfaithful. Gemini makes him intensely curious, he is impulsive and rebellious within himself and he is bored very easily. Aquarians have numerous affairs and are perfectly capable of having more than one paramour at the same time. There is often something highly unusual or original about their romances; their partners may be exotic or bizarre or they may have very strange arrangements in their affairs, meeting in clandestine places or even living in groups. Aquarians are polite and charming lovers, exciting company, and can flatter lovers in the most original and delighting ways. They are also cool, fickle, unfaithful, and can have an affair with the next-door neighbour's wife or suggest a threesome without batting an eylid. Partners of Aquarians will know very soon in their entanglements what they have let themselves in for.

SIXTH HOUSE (WORK/SERVICE)
Ruler Cancer

Cancer's influence, given the versatility of Aquarius, can work in many ways. This is because Cancer is ruled by the Moon, and Cancer can be moody and changeable, just as Aquarius is unpredictable. So, all kinds of things can come from this combination.

Aquarius can, if things go well, be sensitive to the emotional needs of others at work and can satisfy these. Given his practical, ingenious side, he can create an excellent living for himself by doing this – and it can even be by doing something as simple as being a chef, cooking food which satisfies others' appetites (there is always an emotional quality involved in eating food – Cancer knows this well enough). Also, Aquarius may find it congenial to work from home (Cancer again) or to work with his family. Then again, the Cancer influence can make Aquarius emotionally sensitive to those he works *with* and treat them as if they were members of the family. With Aquarius, there's no set formula. All these things are possible.

However, the element of service to others will affect Aquarius. His work, given Cancer's influence, may involve working for the public benefit in some way, in local government or charity organizations or as a public employee. Cancer *does* want to feel that it can serve others (sixth house) in some maternal or protecting way and there is usually something of this influence in what Aquarius chooses to do. An Aquarius can be very effective as a servant to others, because he is cool and practical and not over-sentimental about things.

The Cancer rulership of the sixth tells us something important about Aquarius' health – emotional upsets are the major cause of ill-health for him. However, given his generally rather unemotional nature, he should have generally good health – getting angry or upset by work problems or quarrels may be the one difficulty for him. If such difficulties do arise, Aquarius shouldn't leave them unresolved, because fretting over them can affect health.

SEVENTH HOUSE (MARRIAGE/PARTNERSHIPS)
Ruler Leo

This is where the Leo factor only seems to work in one half of the picture. So far as close partnerships are concerned, Leo's compelling influence clearly does affect Aquarius. Aquarius *needs* others, especially to develop his ideas with. These people are very valuable to him, and he has a deep need for them. He isn't too emotional about it, on the surface, but he has a deep pride in his close friends, and he seeks people with Leo qualities – strong personalities, with real leadership potential, and maybe a touch of the dramatic and larger-than-life about them. Aquarius wants these people to help develop and project his own ideas. Aquarius is too independent, though, to let such people dominate him as Leo people might. Aquarius has a healthy ego and energy and initiative, and that's what he wants from close friends – maybe there's a bit of old-fashioned narcissism in him here.

Where the Leo factor interpretation breaks down – at least in part – is in Aquarius' marriage. Aquarius does take pride in close romantic partners and he can be rather bossy to them – Leo attributes, indeed – but there is no way the loyal steadfast quality of Leo applies to the Aquarian. As we've seen, Aquarians are fickle and rather cool in their affections. They maintain a strong sense of independence in all their affairs. Here, for once, the Leo factor does *not* dominate the Aquarian.

EIGHTH HOUSE (NEEDS FROM OTHERS)
Ruler Virgo

Aquarius can put his ingenious and interesting ideas into good practical shape when it comes to persuading others. He will often do this through partnerships, by working with someone else as a team to develop and refine an idea and get the practical details right. Often, their family partners may help with expanding the family income. There's always a happy knack Aquarius has of getting some really useful practical hints, about little things, from people around him – family, friends, business partners, casual acquaintances, people on the train – he just is lucky this way. This is another reason why Aquarius' sociability tends to be very fortunate for him. Aquarius should keep track of people who are helpful to him and cultivate their company. Their help can be very useful to him at work.

Virgo's influence also explains, in part, why Aquarius is a cool customer; Virgo is a dry, unemotional sign and Aquarius doesn't make a song and dance about expressing his needs. Again, with the combination of Virgo and cool Aquarius, we're talking about material and not emotional needs here. Aquarius rarely *has* emotional needs which require conveying to others. And he's quite happy with this.

NINTH HOUSE (FAR HORIZONS)
Ruler Libra

And yet another reason why Aquarius is a sociable creature. Libra, loving company as it does, influences the house of imagination, and so even with his most inspired imaginings and insights (and there are plenty of them) Aquarius wants to work them through with other people. He usually has good instincts as to whom to choose for this, too, and he's fair in working with them; credits are given where they are due. Aquarius doesn't hog the credit for things, he shares it fairly with others.

If there's weakness here, it is the typical Libran one of wanting things too easy. Although Aquarius can project his ideas forcefully, and he does have a good idea who could be of help, he may be lazy in approaching those people, expecting them to come to him. Aquarius will have to make an effort. He has it going for him – he can express himself clearly and well and he's not without persuasive talents – but he must make that effort.

Aquarians have a strong sense of fairness and justice given this Libran influence. The ninth house (associated with the ninth sign Sagittarius) concerns altruism and lofty ideals and Libra's sense of balance and fair play usually affects Aquarians strongly. And to balance their usual creative concern with *things*, this Libran influence makes them more concerned with *people*. Lastly, Libra makes Aquarians somewhat more amenable to discussion, and readier to understand other people's points of view, than they might be otherwise. Still, it's often true that they may be like this when in conversation but, within themselves, they hold stubborn and steadfast to their own ideas.

TENTH HOUSE (CAREER)
Ruler Scorpio

Scorpio gives Aquarius great power in his career. Aquarius impresses others strongly with the forcefulness of his mind. His ideas, if expressed correctly, persuade others that he is the man for the job. But the trap for Aquarius is using this power too much. Remember that Aries rules the third house of communicating; Aquarius can be pushy, aggressive and overwhelming. If this happens, he will put people's backs up and they will reject him. He has to learn that the secret of Scorpio's power is often silent, a *potential* rather than direct use; people respond to the charisma of this hidden, latent power better than they do if it is unleashed on them. Aquarius does not have to push; he only has to be himself.

Career is crucial to Aquarius on two counts. First, he has to express his ideas, and he may do this in very original, forthright or even revolutionary ways. Second, as well as expressing himself, one aspect of Scorpio is strongly involved. Aquarius develops as a person, transforms and changes himself, through his career. His career life and his personal life at its deepest level are often one and the same. Aquarius knows this (at least subconsciously) and this may be one of the reasons why he's so pushy about himself sometimes. But as he grows more at ease with this Scorpio power he can learn to ease off.

Scorpio's secretiveness makes Aquarius paradoxically adept at ferreting out new and unknown things in his work. This is because Aquarius is curious and ingenious and Scorpio gives him intuitive understandings of hidden things. This is surely one of the reasons why he is so successful as an inventor, and why he has such a reputation for ingenuity.

Some Aquarians are dominating and self-willed, pushing others around at work, contrary to popular belief. But many of them are ambitious not for themselves but for their ideas.

A major trap for Aquarians career-wise is to be rebellious and sarcastic concerning traditional career structures and the like. Aquarius can mouth off all too easily about how such-and-such is a waste of time, how so-and-so's bureaucracy is hopelessly inefficient and how old so-and-so should be got rid of because he's past it. Well, all that may be true, but if it reaches the wrong ears Aquarius will get nowhere in his career. He *must* learn who he can afford to express these ideas to and get away with it!

ELEVENTH HOUSE (FRIENDSHIPS)
Ruler Sagittarius

Aquarius is intensely sociable given this influence on him. Sagittarius, talkative, restless and optimistic, makes Aquarius seek out people with these qualities and he really enjoys their company. Aquarius has many friends – both Sagittarius and Aquarius are restless, readily bored and love novelty. Aquarius will also have many *different* friends. He likes bohemian people, ideas people, inspired visionaries, people working in politics or industry and he can even put up with stuffed shirts for a while (although he's probably laughing at them inside himself. Quite right too). But they *must* be interesting to be worth a second visit. Conservative run-of-the-mill types don't suit him at all.

There's another quality Aquarius looks for in many of his friends; unshockability. After all, Aquarius has a rebellious streak and at least some of his friends must be able to handle this. Since Sagittarians are about the best bet on this score, with this sign ruling this house Aquarius should get lucky here.

Aquarius can even develop some of his more profound ideas (Sagittarius) through encounters with casual friends and acquaintances. Some casual remark can trigger off a 'Eureka!' moment for him. It seems paradoxical, but that's the way Aquarius works. After all, who ever made any real progress by relying on logic and consistency? Aquarius understands this. People who can't understand it will not be his friends for long.

It is important for Aquarius to seek friends in many different places, especially through social clubs of many kinds (debating societies, hobbyists' clubs, chess clubs – preferred by Aquarius to more energetic sports – almost anywhere). By doing this, they meet yet more people who can stimulate their ideas and be of help to them. And they enjoy it too!

TWELFTH HOUSE (THE UNCONSCIOUS)
Ruler Capricorn

It certainly isn't the practical side of Capricorn which Aquarians lack in their conscious minds. Rather, it's the careful, conservative, patient side of Capricorn which Aquarius finds hard to develop within himself. Aquarius is rebellious and impetuous and Capricorn's patience is lacking. A process of slow building is not one which Aquarius can really handle. He's mercurial and too restless for this. Capricorn's carefulness with money is also notably lacking in Aquarius. But something of Capricorn helps Aquarius; he does have endurance if not persistence. Aquarius won't be shaken off a problem; he can come back to it on impulse time and time again and eventually he will get somewhere with it. He just lacks the determined, applied effort to do it in one go. Aquarius isn't a man for deadlines.

For many of us, twelfth house forces are easiest to develop within ourselves when we are alone, in solitude, with time to think things over. For Aquarius, this is technically true, but it probably isn't worth the effort. Given his effectiveness in working with others, it's as well to let that Capricorn side and other intuitive talents pick up who can be of practical help with problems and work with them instead. It's quicker and more effective. But it may not be unusual for Aquarius to do this with some secret or hidden element in the project (twelfth house influence); he may work on some part alone (eventually coming into his work group with a portfolio of ideas and amazing everyone) or on a project which is itself secret.

A cool, mercurial and intelligent, sometimes dazzlingly brilliant, sign, Aquarius. Aquarius isn't the kindest heart in the universe but he is fair and honest, and he both needs and likes his friends. What's more, they get amused, informed, charmed, challenged and entertained. This can't be bad, if you can put up with the odd bit of perversity.

Pisces rising

THE FISH

Pisces is the dreamer of the Zodiac. Inspired, almost a visionary, he sees life rather differently from others. He seems almost unaware of the faults of others; he looks for the best in people. He seems so gentle and kind that the rest of us can become as unrealistic about him, putting him on a pedestal, as he is about us. Pisces has a quality of innocence about him, a naïve charm, which can be irresistible. Pisces really does, it seems, hear, see and speak no evil.

Pisces is also very changeable. He's restless and this can be infuriating because he's so vague about everything. He can be quiet, lost in his dreams, fantasizing about something or someone. But although still waters do run deep in Pisces, this Water sign can brew up a storm. Pisces can become very emotional about his ideas and about other people, but the storm is not directed outwards at others. Rather, water comes to Pisces' eyes in torrents of tears. Because he often sees life so differently from the rest of us, we may find it hard to understand him when he's upset.

Pisces is quite impractical in his life. He has little idea of how to put his visions and imaginings in concrete form. But then he has little interest in things; it's primarily people who concern him. And he has an astonishing sensitivity to other people, an empathy which comes close to the telepathic. Pisceans are aware of subtle nuances of other people's expressions; they intuitively understand body language and they sense the things people don't put into words. Lastly, Pisces has a strong affinity with the arts, especially music and theatre.

Pisces' general personality overlay is that of dreamy idealism and concern for other people. This is almost an other-worldly sign, not an easy one to be born under, but capable of the most altruistic behaviour of any Zodiac sign.

SECOND HOUSE (MONEY)
Ruler Aries

Pisceans do, in fact, expend rather a lot of effort in chasing money (they have to, because they spend it freely too). Given Pisces' artistic inclinations, any performing art where he has to burn up physical energy (Aries) is ideal; hence his liking for theatre. It's not that Pisces has a storehouse of inexhaustible physical energy, he doesn't; rather, if he doesn't get physically involved at all he gets irritable and fretful. The Aries energy has to be burned up.

Pisces does have many ideas for money-making but often he chases his own tail, starting something off and not finishing it. Pisces lacks thoroughness and the Aries energy gets dissipated. Also, the financial projects Pisces has often are woolly-minded and unrealistic, but Pisces may bristle somewhat if this is pointed out to him (Aries influence again). Pisces needs others to channel this Aries energy in constructive ways. If Pisces can make a good actor or even theatrical director he does *not* make a good producer. Others must take over that role.

Pisces is given to impulsive spending on beautiful or artistic things. Again, he has to have the help of others in countering this problem. He can't budget too well himself and his partner, bank manager or just a good friend will have to help him out.

THIRD HOUSE (COMMUNICATING)
Ruler Taurus

Taurus' influence on the third house is another reason why Pisces is inclined to the artistic; Taurus too loves beautiful and artistic things and Pisces wants to communicate his ideas about such things. And he may not be too clear-headed in expressing himself but he does at least have a graceful and charming manner. In particular, Pisceans often have delightful body language, gesturing expressively and using their hands to emphasize what they're saying.

But, oddly enough, Pisceans can be rather stubborn creatures where their ideas are concerned. Taurus is a steadfast sign and, as we'll see, their ninth house affairs make them rather fixed and stubborn too. They can be rather intense about their ideas and they don't change them easily. Attempting to change Pisces' mind with logical argument is a complete waste of time. Pisces does not respond to arguments of this type. Someone trying to persuade him by using the language of poetry, metaphors, possibilities – well, that's different, but some dry stick with a liking for cold logic – never. Pisces does not understand logic but he does understand parables.

Pisceans are slow in forming their ideas (Pisces is woolly-minded and Taurus is hardly quick on the uptake), which may be one of the reasons why they're so stubborn about them when they have made their minds up about something. A pitfall for Pisces is that he may be lazy about communicating (Taurus again) and retreat into his dream-world rather than make the effort to talk with people who may not understand him too readily. He simply has to make the effort to find which friends do respond to him, the ones he *can* talk to.

FOURTH HOUSE (HOME)
Ruler Gemini

Gemini's restless influence means that there is little stability in the home life of Pisceans. They may travel away from home a lot, keep two homes if they can afford it, change their home base often, move around from time to time. Pisces' home life can be rather chaotic.

However, Pisces' home is an interesting place; Gemini is never boring. Pisces is likely to cram it with art objects, and above all books given Gemini's intellectual influence. Pisces may enjoy using his home as a base for intellectual life and conversation; he will enjoy having friends around with whom he can exchange his ideas and he may feel happier and more secure doing it here than anywhere else.

Piscean children may benefit from the Gemini influence, or things may go wrong. If they're lucky, their parents are intelligent, clever and tolerant people who understand the young Piscean and help him to express himself better and feel more secure. But Gemini's restlessness can give the young Piscean a lack of stability in his home, moving too often and impairing his schooling or even a divorce lurking in the background. Such things puzzle and hurt the child.

Piscean parents may be uniquely gifted with their children. Their love of their offspring is great and the Gemini influence enables them to capture the imagination of their child by telling him wonderful stories built from their own imaginations and Gemini's ability to express itself. Piscean parents must be the best in the Zodiac for nurturing the child's sense of wonder at the world around him. And all Piscean family members are likely to keep well in touch with each other, writing and phoning frequently, and they need this.

Pisceans should realize that often they can best express themselves and develop their ideas most easily when at home. Since they tend to be rather seclusive anyway, many of them may have already figured this out by now!

FIFTH HOUSE (CREATIVITY)
Ruler Cancer

Cancer's emotional nature pushes Pisces even further in his creativity towards concerns about people. Pisces could never be an inventor or mechanical genius; he is concerned with people and their feelings. Whatever he dreams up, it will always be directly concerned with people.

But the main emphasis of Cancer's influence is in Pisces' romantic life, which is not easy but which is very intense. Pisces is very sensitive to the moods of others given Cancer's receptivity, and he responds to all the changing moods of anyone with whom he's emotionally close. Pisces is an incorrigible romancer. He loves his partner deeply, endlessly and with a complete disregard for any of the practicalities of life (at least to begin with). He is very emotional about his loved one and cries easily at any upset. He over-idealizes his partner easily, and when he's in love his whole world revolves around this. But because he is so very easily upset, and because he's so idealistic and indeed a bit of a perfectionist where his partner is concerned, his heart breaks easily. It is very hard for Pisces to draw back and be light-hearted about his loves; and it's also hard for him to allow his loved one enough independence (Cancer wants to know what's going on. It's too protective to be otherwise).

Given the Cancer link with parents — especially the mother — Pisceans may often fall for people who remind them of their parents. This is especially true with Piscean men, who have something of a mother complex about them. The problem, of course, is that Pisces may be falling in love with an image he's projecting onto that other person rather than with the person herself. But Pisces is far too impractical to tell the difference or even be aware of the problem most of the time.

Pisceans do not usually have easy romantic lives, but if and when they do get it right and find the right person they are ecstatic. They walk on air and the whole world seems filled with love and affection to them. Pisceans know only extremes in their love affairs.

SIXTH HOUSE (WORK/SERVICE)
Ruler Leo

The Leo factor in Pisces influences the sixth house, and usually it's the element of service to others the Leo factor affects. Pisces yearns to be doing something good for humanity. He almost wants to sacrifice himself through work to help other people. This can be in almost any way, from direct help (in charities or organizations helping political prisoners or virtually anything of this sort) to doing something to make people's lives richer and better (like acting). Pisces takes great pride in this, yet he does not have any of the arrogance of Leo about him. Simply, he feels a whole person with a sense of purpose in his life when he's doing something for others like this.

However, for some Pisces people the Leo factor does make them surprisingly dominant over others at work. This is not the actor but the theatrical director. Pisces still wants to be doing something useful for others but now the Leo influence makes him want to organize and direct others to do it as well. This can be a tremendously effective role for Pisces. Although he will dominate others, with his lack of arrogance or selfishness and hs sensitivity to the moods and feelings of others he can become admired and loved by those work for him.

It is crucial for Pisceans to know which of these roles they're best suited for, because Leo's drive is so strong they *must* get this right. Career advice people can be vital for Pisceans. They need to know the details and practical side of career life, because they rarely grasp such details unaided. Since Pisceans often latch onto practical and established people at work, this may not be too difficult for them. People with many years' experience in an area of work Pisceans are interested in should be approached for the help they can give. Pisceans simply *must* do this.

SEVENTH HOUSE (MARRIAGE/PARTNERSHIPS)
Ruler Virgo

In marriage, Pisces *may* be lucky with this Virgo influence. He may be attracted to, and marry, someone who has the practical gifts of Virgo and who can work with him to put his dreams into useable form. Such a partner may be hardworking and efficient and Pisces will, as usual, idealize them and adore them for these virtues.

On the other hand, Pisces may find that he has a shrew on his hands – a nagging, nit-picking persons who criticizes him and makes him unhappy. He still loves that person but his life is really rather a misery. Either way, Pisces will often attract someone who is rather exacting about him. He does rather need this, but he can live without the nagging.

In business partnerships Pisces may be fortunate. He may fall in with people with Virgo virtues, who can work with him, supplying the attention to detail and practical considerations which he can't manage. Pisces needs people like this. They can often be quite cool, careful people (Virgo again), very different to Pisces' emotional nature, but he can recognize his need for them and work happily with them.

EIGHTH HOUSE (NEEDS FROM OTHERS)
Ruler Libra

Libra's influence affects the way Pisces expresses his needs to others and the reactions he gets from them. Libra certainly gives Pisces charm – one of the reasons for his grace in expressing himself – but Libra's laziness added to Pisces' occasional lack of coherence can make for a rather indolent, offhand person. People don't take him very seriously, although he offends no-one and everyone likes him. He's just ineffectual.

Libra's affinity with working with others shows that Pisces is best advised to work with other people to get his ideas and needs across. This is especially true where money is concerned. Pisceans do indeed enjoy doing this and it's a relief to leave the practicalities to others.

Emotionally, Libra gives Pisces great charm and reinforces his altruism. Libra is a lover of fairness and even dealing and Pisces wants to better the lot of humanity. A prime need Pisces has, then, is the need to make things better for others; altruism, humanitarian concerns. Given Libra's involvement, we can see why other people are often touched by this and love Pisces for it. We may not respect his formidable mind but we know his heart is very much in the right place.

As well as working with others, Pisces usually understands that he can get what he wants simply by being who he is — a kind, affectionate person. People respond to this. Pisces rarely has to push for what he wants, but he has to avoid the typical Libran pitfall of being too lazy. The secret for Pisces lies in making sure he's in circulation enough socially to get noticed.

NINTH HOUSE (FAR HORIZONS)
Ruler Scorpio

So, of course, Pisces is a dreamer. He couldn't be anything else with Scorpio ruling this house. Two typical qualities of Scorpio affect Piscean imagination. First, the sheer power of Scorpio. Pisces is a fluent dreamer and his imaginings are endless; the force of Scorpio is rather dissipated because of the untogetherness of Pisces, so Scorpio doesn't help with making the ideas more practical or better thought-out, but the energies still stimulate the flow of ideas Pisces has. And Scorpio is secretive. Pisces too is rather shy and retiring and he likes to dream alone. Pisces withdraws into himself and lets his mind wander. In his imagination all kinds of beautiful and idealistic things may come to pass. The one blessing Scorpio brings to him above all others is that the Scorpio energy does make him want to *do* something about all this. Otherwise, he'd just stay in his dream world forever.

Scorpio's tenacity also helps explain why Pisceans hold to their ideas with such stubbornness. They can even be crusaders for some religious or political group — not the most effective spokesmen, maybe, but Scorpio's charisma can impress people listening to them. They can be caught out on points of detail or logic but since when were politicians or men of religion bothered about things like this? And Pisceans can get very angry if their ideas are ridiculed or mocked. The aggressive quality of Scorpio is unleashed. Pisces is usually a gentle Water sign, but there can be storms at sea.

TENTH HOUSE (CAREER)
Ruler Sagittarius

Sagittarius brings Pisces good fortune in his career and sometimes he is able to see career opportunities intuitively and grasp them. Most of the time, though, he needs advice from others, and he needs to work with others more gifted in practical matters than he is (Sagittarius is not a particularly practical sign). Pisces wants his work to be useful to others, of course – there are already enough reasons for that and Sagittarius' philanthropy adds to them.

Pisceans can make excellent teachers given Sagittarius' rulership of the tenth house. They are superb teachers of the young, stimulating their imaginations and conveying ideas and a love of beauty and fairness to them. And they may teach other people in many ways – a fine actor is teaching us something through his ability to portray a character brilliantly and with emotional force.

Pisceans impracticality with career lives can lead them into problems because Sagittarius is even more restless and changing that Pisces itself. Pisces may chop and change from one job to another, never really making any progress in any sphere of his work life. It helps Pisceans if they have hobbies or even second jobs of some kind to stop them getting bored at work. They *will* get bored from time to time because they're moody, and again flexible hours or working from home are good options for them. They need to be able to drop things for a while and return when they feel refreshed and enthusiastic again. These strategies are much better for a Piscean than trying to tell himself to knuckle down and get on with it. He can't do this, and his mind will simply wander off at tangents and he'll get increasingly bored and irritable.

ELEVENTH HOUSE (FRIENDSHIPS)
Ruler Capricorn

The positive side of this is that Pisces may well find that he attracts friends who help him out in practical ways. Capricorn's very practical nature helps Pisces; his intuitions are balanced by Capricorn-like friends. Obviously, that's very helpful to him at work. Such people are often older than the Piscean and in a position of established authority. They may be a little stern with him from time to time, which makes him feel depressed or anxious, but their influence is good overall.

The negative side is that, socially, Pisces may find his friends are a burden to him. There is a gloomy, negative side to Capricorn and since Pisces is emotionally sensitive he may find that his friends' problems also weigh heavily on him. Poor Pisces is attracted to suffering people, but he may find that their unhappiness brings him down too. Then he can't function himself, since he's too unhappy, and he withdraws into himself. Pisces can almost seem to be a masochist. He needs to learn that he can't deal with all his friends' problems, much as he'd like to, and he cannot carry the burden of all their emotional hurts around with him. Pisces will have to concentrate on only a few friends and try to be of help with them. Actually, he is really not too bad at that, since Capricorn's practical side helps him and his empathy with others communicates itself. Pisces wants to help everyone, but he will have to settle for just a few so far as his friends go.

TWELFTH HOUSE (THE UNCONSCIOUS)
Ruler Aquarius

One aspect of the hidden, buried Aquarius side is obvious in Pisces. Aquarius can be detached about people, and it has 'objective' qualities; Aquarius is very interested in things rather than people. Pisces is the exact reverse of all this. Pisces finds it very difficult to look at problems in anything other than an emotional way. The Aquarian detachment is quite absent from him. Likewise, Pisces is seclusive while Aqaurius is very gregarious. Pisces *is* very concerned with others but often at a distance except where friends are concerned, and he is often shy and nervous with people doesn't know. Most un-Aquarian.

Twelfth house forces are usually easiest to draw out of oneself alone. But Pisces is strongly given to daydreaming alone, rather than drawing out this Aquarian detachment and cool logic. It is a very difficult side of himself to develop, but it has to be: many of Pisces' problems come from the fact that he is too strongly emotionally attached to others. While this is noble, it doesn't make him any more clear-headed and he can suffer badly on account of it.

What does come through more readily from the Aquarian side is the intuitive, brilliant, inspirational aspect of that sign. That is in keeping with Pisces' general personality. But the Aquarian ability to make those insights work is lacking in Pisces. Still, Aquarius' gregarious nature, coupled with Pisces' sensitivity, is a powerful mix: no surprise that Pisces is hypersensitive to others, even mediumistic or telepathic. Pisces is subliminally aware of many things about other people; he often can't put this knowledge into words but he shows us his understanding in the ways he looks at us and expresses concern.

A major trap for Pisces – again coming from the Aquarian affinity with the eleventh house and friendship – is that he can be a major burden to his friends by continually harping on about his unhappiness and problems in life. This is the exact mirror-image of the problem Capricorn's rulership of the eleventh house can create. This all underlines the point that Pisces must choose his friends carefully. A friend who can be light-hearted and take Pisces' mind off gloomy subjects by enthusiastically and happily talking with him about things he loves – music, art, travel and so on – is a godsend for him.

☆ ☆ ☆

This last of the 12 Zodiac signs is, maybe, the most extreme and difficult of all to be born under. Pisceans almost seem to live in a different world from everyone else. They're so impractical, about virtually everything, that it's almost unbelievable; one is tempted to lose patience with them completely. This would be a huge mistake. No-one is capable of such service to other people, such complete unselfishness, as Pisceans. Intuitive, inspirational and almost child-like, Pisceans almost shame the rest of us with their affection and concern. If only we can help them make that concern work.

Part Three

RISING SIGNS
AND SUN SIGNS

Rising signs and Sun signs

When someone knows both their Rising signs and Sun sign, an astrologer can tell much more about them from knowing both than from knowing only one. The Rising sign gives more information – as we've seen, it tells us about a general 'overlay' in the personality, a set of characteristics which influence more or less everything the person does. The Sun sign tells us more about the emotional heart of the person, although we can learn something about that from the 'Leo factor' from the Rising sign – the house which Leo rules.

Putting together Rising and Sun signs obviously gives 144 possible combinations, and it's impossible to consider them all individually here. The easiest way to look at combinations is to group them into 16 types; these 16 come from the four times four permutations of the signs arranged in groups according to the astrological element they're associated with. If this all sounds a bit formidable, to refresh your memory here are the signs and elements:

Fire   Aries, Leo, Sagittarius
Water   Cancer, Scorpio, Pisces
Air   Gemini, Libra, Aquarius
Earth   Taurus, Virgo, Capricorn

and, again, the essential psychology of the elements:

Fire   Passion, energy, enthusiasm
Water   Emotion, intuition, sensitivity
Air   Thinking, intelligence, communicating
Earth   Solidity, endurance, 'building'

Of the 16 possible combinations (Rising sign in Fire + Sun sign in Fire, Rising sign in Fire + Sun sign in Water, and so on), four are 'doubles' – when the Rising sign and Sun sign are both in the same element. When this is the case, the psychology of the person is very strongly typical of that element. The double-Fire person is a fireball, a tremendously energetic and enthusiastic person; the double-Water Person a highly sensitive, very emotional person, the double-Air person a real intellectual, highly expressive and intelligent, and the double-Earth person very conservative, cautious, prudent, and practical. For people like this, the general personality overlay will be very much reinforced; the Rising sign described in Part 2 of this book will describe them very accurately. And this is especially true when the Rising sign and the Sun sign are exactly the same, so that one had a double-Aries, double-Taurus or whatever. An important point is that, with such people, the Rising sign description given earlier will not only be highly accurate but, when there is any conflict between the general influence of the Rising sign and a specific influence of another sign ruling one of the other 11 houses, the conflict will always be resolved in favour of the Rising sign influence. One example: Sagittarians, inclined to be spendthrift, have Capricorn – careful and prudent – ruling the second house. Capricorn wants to scrimp and save and its influence rules the second house of money. Usually Sagittarians have some conflicts about money given this, but if the person is a double-Sagittarian they are spendthrift for sure and to hell with Capricorn. If you are a double, re-read your Rising sign description keeping this in mind.

Which leaves us 12 groups of Rising sign/Sun sign combinations, which we can look at.

RISING SIGN IN FIRE + SUN SIGN IN AIR
Aries/Leo/Sagittarius + Gemini/Libra/Aquarius

The key principle here is *thought into action*. Air and Fire is a harmonious mix; Fire's flames leap in Air and its love of freedom isn't constrained. Air enjoys the leaping response of Fire, and Fire makes Air move. This person is basically unemotional; carefully considers; but their thoughts and ideas have to be put across to others. A Fire-Air person won't be happy sitting around intellectualizing or doing crosswords; the store of ideas has *got* to be expressed directly. Such a person wants to get his ideas through to you face-to-face so that his Fire enthusiasm can be used to the full.

The airy Sun sign makes Rising Arians, Leos and Sagittarians more intellectual than they'd otherwise be (this is especially true for Aries and Leo; Sagittarius is an intellectual sign anyway). It gives them greater abilities for self-criticism and standing back and thinking about what they're doing. This influence is especially strong if the Sun sign is Gemini; a Libran Sun makes the person more laid-back about life in general and their passions in particular and an Aquarian Sun can make them ingenious, even brilliant.

The Fire-Air combination contains three polar opposites where the Sun and Rising signs are in direct opposition; Aries–Libra, Gemini–Sagittarius and Leo–Aquarius. We'll take a more detailed look at those later.

RISING SIGN IN FIRE+SUN SIGN IN EARTH
Aries/Leo/Sagittarius+Taurus/Virgo/Capricorn

They key principle here is *energetic building*; this person has the Earth drive to construct and develop practical things and the Fire side of him has the energy and enthusiasm to do it. He may also be very adept at galvanizing other people into getting things done with him. This Fire-Earth combination can work fairly well; Fire is 'on the surface' and still feels free. The Earth side of the person may be a little strained (Fire scorches Earth) but most of the time this pairing can be successful. The Fire side can bring more urgency and more pleasure into the life of a person with an Earth Sun sign. Even the more unlikely looking combinations can work: a Rising Sagittarius with a Capricorn Sun, for example, leaves the Capricorn Sun happily placed in the second house of money. Things work out!

The Earth Sun gives the person with a fiery Rising sign more solidity, endurance and reliability. This is most pronounced with Sagittarians and, to a lesser extent, with Leos, who can be rather lazy; the Earth influence will make them more industrious. If there are problems it can be with a potential for exhaustion through doing too much; the Earth person works hard but not usually that fast while the Fire side of him is so enthusiastic it demands constant effort. This is especially true with an Arian Rising sign.

RISING SIGN IN FIRE+SUN SIGN IN WATER
Aries/Leo/Sagittarius+Cancer/Scorpio/Pisces

Most of these combinations are, bluntly, fairly disastrous. Fire hates Water; Water is the element which destroys and engulfs it. Likewise, Fire turns Water to steam and destroys it in their meeting; this is OK by Pisces (since it's a fairly volatile sign anyway) but not by Cancer or Scorpio. There is restlessness and agitation with this mix and the key principle is one of *restless conflict*. Fire's restlessness makes this sort of person agitated and rather nervous, because of the emotionality of the Water Sun sign. Their apparent restlessness conceals conflict and emotional agitation. The emotion of Water and the energies of Fire create anxiety, a feeling of insecurity; a Fire-Water person can't be at peace within themselves and neither can they keep quiet with others (Fire won't let them). They lack concentration and persistence (except, perhaps, where Scorpio is involved together with Aries or Leo) and they feel they badly want to express their ideas and emotions (the two usually run together for them), but can't do so easily or coherently.

The conflicts which Fire and Water can produce can lead to anything from a very scatty, untogether person (the Pisces/Sagittarius mix being the worst) to a violent, anxious personality with real inner turmoil (Aries/Scorpio would be the worst here). This combination is the worst of all possible ones, I'm afraid, and there are no easy answers to the problems Fire/Water people face.

RISING SIGN IN AIR+SUN SIGN IN FIRE
Gemini/Libra/Aquarius+Aries/Leo/Sagittarius

This combination is 'hotter' than when the Rising sign is in Air and the Sun sign in Fire. The key principle of this sign is *energy communicated*. The fiery heart of the person feels strongly about his ideals, and the Air rising sign gives him the intellectual abilities to put those views across. This makes the biggest difference to Aries and Leo; neither is an intellectual sign but the airy Rising sign brings skills in thinking and communicating with others.

This combination is harmonious, and powerful. The Air-Fire person is not cool; no-one with a Fire heart is, and he uses the mental skills Air brings him to express what he *feels*. And the airy Rising sign may increase the restlessness of such a person, especially when Gemini is involved. His ideas and views have to be put over to many, and different, people.

The Air-Fire person is swift, courageous and decisive. However, this combination can be rather aggressive and critical in speech, especially if either Aries or Aquarius is involved. Air-Fire may not be kindly to those who are not as gifted in speech and thinking and it can pour scorn on more emotionally sensitive people and the tender-hearted; this is not a mixture of elements which makes someone sentimental, unless Libra is the Air sign involved.

Again, as with Fire-Air, the Air-Fire mix contains three oppositions of Rising and Sun signs, and we'll look at those later.

RISING SIGN IN AIR+SUN SIGN IN EARTH
Gemini/Libra/Aquarius+Taurus/Virgo/Capricorn

This combination can work well. The key principle is that of *constructive thinking*. Earth signs are not, usually, particularly intelligent (save for Virgo) and the airy Rising sign compensates for that. The person with the Earth Sun has practical and constructive ideas, and the Air Rising sign allows them to express these well. The Gemini Rising sign can make for someone who is really something of an inventive genius if given the chance, when an Earth Sun is involved.

What is striking about the Air-Earth combination as opposed to other types of Rising sign paired with an Earth Sun is that these people can think well on their feet and their reactions under pressure can be intelligent and creative. Given a problem they can find something to help in a practical way in a very short time. It may only be a holding operation but it buys the time for people to find a more permanent solution to the problem. Such speed of mental reactions is very unusual in Earth people.

Still, Air and Earth are opposed elements and if there is a problem here it is because Air is confined and almost feels trapped by the solidity of Earth. These people may feel a sense of insecurity or restlessness because they are not developing the more intellectual side of their personalities while working on the practical problems they're so good at. It is important for Air-Earth people to take time off from all those practical concerns and read widely, cultivate intelligent friends and generally avoid the 'all work and no play' syndrome.

RISING SIGN IN AIR+SUN SIGN IN WATER
Gemini/Libra/Aquarius+Cancer/Scorpio/Pisces

Oddly enough, this unpromising combination can work – sometimes. After all, Air is volatile, and so is Water (Pisces most so, Scorpio least so). The emotional quality of the Water Sun colours the person's thinking and expressions and such a person can be graceful, artistic, able to communicate their emotional ideas through art, television, video or other media where their presentation and graceful expression can come through. These people are often more sociable than Water people usually are, particularly if Libra or Gemini is involved (and Pisces isn't).

Air-Water people often have a strong sense of aesthetics, and strong personal eithical codes. They argue for their beliefs more coherently, given the Air rising sign, than Water people usually can. They are often fascinated by religion, philosophy, the paranormal, any area of 'nonrational' knowledge where there intuitive understanding can operate and where they can express their ideas freely. Their restlessness can lead them to develop more than one career or to choose jobs which have a great deal of variety, possibly including travel. They are not usually terribly persistent at what they do and work in fits and starts (unless Scorpio is the Water sign involved).

The key principle of this Air-Water combination is *emotional thinking*; instead of saying 'I think that . . .' they would, if we had a word for this in the English language, say 'I feel-think that . . .'.

RISING SIGN IN EARTH+SUN SIGN IN FIRE
Taurus/Virgo/Capricorn+Aries/Leo/Sagittarius

Usually this combination is not a happy one. The heart of Fire feels itself trapped within the solidity of Earth; the energy is bound up and can create a lot of inner tension. This problem is greatest when Sagittarius or Capricorn are involved; the combination of Sagittarius and Virgo, though, is perhaps least difficult. The key principle here can be one of *trapped energy*.

Fire's activity and urgency wants to do things and not to be tied down; this Earth-Fire person can be frustrated by having to deal in terms of practicalities all the time, or being unable to express their ideas as cleverly as they'd like (Earth not being given to intelligent, witty speaking). The burden on Fire can thus be internal (lack of ability to shine in speech and expressing ideas) or external (family duties, a deadening career, etc.).

Earth-Fire people almost always do feel frustrated or unfulfilled in some way because the Earth part of them keeps the Fire part too much in check and this keeps their passions and desires unexpressed, or only badly expressed. This creates anxiety, tension or even violence (especially if Aries is involved). It may be crucial for such people to find some demanding project where they have *plenty of time* to think things through and get them done. The Fire part of them needs some major challenge and the Earth part needs the time; the project can be anything the Fire part feels positive about and responds to, from travelling round the world to building the neighbourhood's biggest greenhouse. It just has to be something that satisfies Fire's urge to do something *big*, and if the project involves burning up physical energy, so much the better.

RISING SIGN IN EARTH+SUN SIGN IN AIR
Taurus/Virgo/Capricorn+Gemini/Libra/Aquarius

This combination doesn't usually work either, unless Libra is the Air sign involved. The problem is similar to the Earth-Fire mix: the heart of the person struggles for intellectual expression, for getting ideas across cleverly and persuasively, but the Earth Rising sign doesn't provide the intelligence or speed of thinking for this. There may be problems for such people imposed externally through inadequate education, or parental failure to provide for the natural curiosity of the child. What's more, if Virgo is involved such a person can be very self-critical, making for an unhappy time of it.

Earth-Air people have to work hard at developing the ability to communicate their ideas as expansively as they'd like; that can mean anything from reading widely to build up a store of knowledge useful in conversations to meeting others in encounter groups (really!). They *can* put across ideas in a practical way but they want more than this; they want to be able to sparkle a little in conversation, and amuse and challenge other people.

Earth-Air people often have an inner restlessness because they don't trust their own ideas, feeling they may not be practical enough, and they may be uncomfortable with playing ideas around or indulging in lateral thinking, even though this is just what the Air part of them wants and what they need to develop.

The key principle here can be one of *unfulfilled intellect* and it can be a lifetime's work to put that straight.

RISING SIGN IN EARTH+SUN SIGN IN WATER
Taurus/Virgo/Capricorn+Cancer/Scorpio/Pisces

Usually this combination is harmonious. Earth-Water people are passive, intuitive, sensitive to others but they are able to express their emotional concern for others in practical ways given the Earth Rising sign. The combination is certainly most harmonious when Scorpio isn't the Water sign involved. The key principle here is one of *practical emotional awareness*. Both Water and Earth are passive elements and not outgoing, but the Earth Rising sign gives the ability to *do* things effectively and the Water Sun sign gives the person the awareness of, and concern for, other people and their feelings. This is an excellent combination for those working in counselling, psychotherapy, marriage guidance, nursing – any career where sensitivity to other people's emotions and the ability to act on intuitive, sensitive reactions to them are involved.

This combination can, in fortunate people, give inspirational or intuitive gifts of an unequalled kind. The Water part of such people draws them to art, religion, philosophical and social concerns; the Earth part gives them the talents to put their insights into effective action. Great actors, social reformers, musicians, artists and similar people may often have this Earth-Water combination.

Lastly, the Earth-Water mix contains three oppositions (Taurus-Scorpio, Cancer-Capricorn and Virgo-Pisces) and we'll look at these in detail later.

RISING SIGN IN WATER+SUN SIGN IN FIRE
Cancer/Scorpio/Pisces+Aries/Leo/Sagittarius

Fire and Water simply don't mix and this combination is not a good one. Fire's passions are trapped within the element which destroys it and its energies are dissipated and lost. Water-Fire people certainly badly want to *do* things but they are usually confused as to exactly what and have little idea of how to do what they want even if they manage to figure things out. There is a conflict between the boisterous, extrovert nature of Fire and the sensitive moody and shy nature of Water; these people want to be gregarious and the life and soul of the party but their perceptions of other people's moods, emotions and occasional unhappiness is too great for this. Extroverts, after all, need to be somewhat thick-skinned and the Water Rising sign is anything but. There can be much frustration inside Water-Fire people on this score; they feel unfulfilled in their relationships with other people. They would like to be sociable and happy-go-lucky but it can't be done.

So, what often happens is that Fire's energies get trapped within the person and converted into anxiety and tension. As with any person with Fire in their make-up, physical burning-off of the energy can be important.

Some of these combinations (especially when Scorpio is involved) can be surprisingly cruel or even sadistic given the unfulfilled inner longings of Fire; the tension is projected outwards as aggression or destructiveness. With the intuitive understanding of other's emotions and weak points which Water has, this can be quite devastating. This is not a good combination of elements in any way; the key principle is one of *frustrated energy*. It's a more volatile combination than that of Earth and Fire, and the energy isn't just trapped – it's frustrated, still volatile and operates in negative ways for the most part.

RISING SIGN IN WATER+SUN SIGN IN AIR
Cancer/Scorpio/Pisces+Gemini/Libra/Aquarius

This is a double-edged mix; the combination can be good or bad. The key principle is one of *intuitive thinking*; Water-Air people can be powerful individuals.

When this combination works, the person is able to sense the feelings, thoughts and reactions of others through the Water Rising sign and yet stand back from it and analyse what's going on (the airy Sun). Such people may have strong ethical and personal standards, from the influence of Water on their thinking, and they can express their interest in and concern for others in brilliant and inventive ways. They can communicate concern effectively, and they can be cool and considered about how to deal with personal and social problems. A strong combination.

But there can be a secretive, even brooding, side to this, especially when Scorpio is involved; the Water-Air person can be deceitful, an emotional parasite, even cruel. They use their awareness of others to benefit themselves in cold and calculating ways. This is unusual, though, except where Scorpio is involved. The Water-Air combination can lack practicality; the ideas can feel right and be put over in dazzling ways but they can't work. This is especially true when Pisces or, to a lesser extent, Aquarius is involved (the combination is quite appalling on this score).

RISING SIGN IN WATER+SUN SIGN IN EARTH
Cancer/Scorpio/Pisces+Taurus/Virgo/Capricorn

This is the most passive of all combinations. It is a kindly, affectionate, concerned mix; Water-Earth people are sensitive to other people and offer help unselfishly. The Earth Rising sign gives the ability to do this in practical ways and it makes such people less unpredictable than Water people usually are. It is not a combination which makes for high intelligence, but it is very intuitive. These people don't need dazzling wit and conversation; they *know* what is going on because they *feel* it and they can express their understanding in ways which may be simple and direct but which can say more to another person than a thousand brilliant sentences of conversation. The key principle here is one of *compassionate feeling*, even when Scorpio is involved; these people are the least selfish imaginable.

Water-Earth people simply know how to say the right things to unhappy friends and they never push their own views; they only suggest or give hints. Their main concern is to express fellow-feeling and give comfort. They quite lack aggression (Scorpio's influence may simply make them more shy and introverted) and they may have problems because of that, getting stepped on by more callous people because they lack assertiveness. Anyone stepping on Water-Earth people has to be a real villain; this is a noble and kindly combination. Like Earth and Water, there are three oppositions here too, and now we can look at these.

Oppositions

SUN AND RISING SIGNS DIRECTLY OPPOSED

When astrologers compute complete horoscopes, oppositions are often taken as difficult aspects of the personality; two planets placed 180° apart in the wheel of the Zodiac show aspects of the person in conflict. However, this is the traditional view; some modern astrologers dispute this, and so far as Sun and Rising signs go, oppositions don't necessarily mean conflict. This is because, as we saw in Part 1 of the book, the 12 signs form related pairs, the opposed signs complement each other, the last six being in some sense more outgoing or 'deeper' versions of the first six. So the oppositions may be harmonious and work well; as a general rule, if the Sun sign is in the 7th to 12th signs (Libra to Pisces) and the Rising sign in the 1st to 6th (Aries to Virgo) there is greater harmony than when the reverse is true. This is because the 7th–12th Sun sign gives a 'core' personality which is more altruistic and less concerned with personal matters than a 1st–6th Sun sign, and the more personal ways of expressing oneself the 1st–6th Rising sign brings provides the ways of putting 'deeper' concerns and interests across effectively as an individual. But the reverse picture isn't necessarily negative either, as we'll see.

ARIES–LIBRA

This opposition is *not* an easy one. It's better for the person concerned, perhaps, if the Sun is in Aries and the Rising sign is Libra. With this mix, the standard Aries problem – of being too pushy for it's own good – is countered by Libra's engaging and charming manner. Now the aggressive Aries can persuade people as well as bulldozing them. The reverse picture can be awkward; the person with the Libra Sun wants to be pleasant and agreeable and have harmony with partners and friends but he's frustrated in this because he has an overbearing or aggressive manner when dealing with them. So that combination isn't ideal personally but it can make for a powerful professional person; the Libran desire for justice and fairness allied to the Arian drive can make for a highly effective social agitator ('This isn't right and it *won't* stay like this!'). Aries counters Libra's laziness and this mix can be powerful indeed.

TAURUS–SCORPIO

Difficult in most cases, this combination. Taurus–Scorpio is an intense person, a powerhouse of energy which can be 'fixed' within the person and create much inner tension. Taurus–Scorpio can be a tremendous worker, and achieve a great deal. There may be a lack of imagination, though, and this is not a highly intelligent combination.

When Scorpio is the Sun sign, the person has the practical gifts to achieve what Scorpio wants – and the emotional awareness of Scorpio coupled with Taurus' fairness can produce a very ethical, gifted worker. Taurus–Scorpio can be a forceful righter of wrongs in society, working as a social worker, therapist, agitator, in many ways. When Taurus is the Sun sign, the vices of this combination may become more evident – we may have a brooding, suspicious and rather aloof person who gets what he wants any way he can.

GEMINI–SAGITTARIUS

This is a splendid mix – in some ways. This must be the most potent communicator imaginable, especially if Sagittarius is the Sun sign. This person can argue the hind legs off a donkey, and if Sagittarius is the Sun sign then he has something worth talking about. Gemini is a more superficial sign than Sagittarius and the Sagittarian Sun gives deeper substance to this combination. Air and Fire usually mix well and this combination is bright, alert, witty and very fast-thinking.

There can, however, be some impracticality about this combination – it's so fond of its own ideas that it chases them around endlessly and doesn't make the effort to put them into practice. Gemini–Sagittarius can be hyperactive, over-restless, and lacking in persistence. But given the formidable mental abilities of this combination, the odds are it will be bright enough to get others to do the hard work. Gemini–Sagittarius will make an excellent executive director in any profession where communicating and ideas are at a premium.

CANCER–CAPRICORN

This is a sensitive, rather passive, intuitive mix. Such people are highly sensitive to others and responsive to their feelings. With a Capricorn Sun, this person is able to develop projects and get things done by enlisting the help of others who find his approaches diplomatic, kindly and fair; Capricorn–Cancer is a highly ethical creature, someone who won't cut corners or take the easy way out unless this is scrupulously fair and harms no-one. Such a person is very gifted at managing people; as personnel directors, or in any job where they're responsible for hiring people or looking after their welfare, they function very effectively and are liked for their fairness.

With a Cancer Sun the emotional, watery side of the partnership is more in evidence and the person may be more inclined towards the caring professions – which they're admirably suited to. The Earth Rising sign makes them very practical in their approach to problems.

The Cancer-Capricorn mix is a very harmonious one; it's faults are a certain lack of imagination, and possibly getting stuck in a rut and being rather dogmatic about the correctness of its own ideas.

LEO–AQUARIUS

This is a more double-edged combination. With a Leo Sun, such a person can be quite ingenious; their personal creativity is intense, since Leo wants to create and do things and Aquarius has the ingenuity to come up with the real flash of insight. But the Aquarian stubbornness can also make this person a dreadful bore; Leo is proud and sometimes arrogant and Aquarius, in its perverse moods, a thorough pain in the neck. The combination can produce a person who believes that he's right about everything and has every intention of announcing this to everyone he can; a dreadful creature.

The Aquarius Sun/Leo Rising sign mix is a little less prone to such anti-social extremes, although the potential is still there. This person is rather cooler, more detached and more prepared to think things over than the person with the Leo Sun and Aquarius Rising sign. It's still a powerfully creative mix and one with fewer rough edges to the personality, a rather more graceful and persuasive mix (but beware the Aquarian cranky moods nonetheless).

Aquarius–Leo does not care for any kind of hard physical work but it is a strong ideas person and good at getting others organized and in any work with new technologies (the Aquarius side). Aquarius–Leo is probably happiest bossing other people about, and he can do this without putting people's backs up – most of the time.

PISCES–VIRGO

This combination isn't easy because of the very different mental nature of the signs – Virgo is cool, critical, very much a thinking sign, occupied with trivia and minor detail, while Pisces is a dreamer, artistic, thinking in terms of symbols and beautiful things, not cold logic or reason. But there are common principles too; both signs are inclined towards being of service to other people, and neither is aggressive or pushy. The combination can work well for other people; Pisces–Virgo is a devoted servant of humanity and may be able to put those Piscean dreams into practical form. This is most likely with a Virgo Sun, because of the greater impracticality of Pisces. The person with the Pisces Sun may be the nobler spirit but the rather less effective planner and worker.

However, there is always conflict within a Pisces–Virgo person. The coolness of Virgo criticizes and mocks the dreaming Pisces and the person may feel very restless, dissatisfied with their inability to express their ideas clearly, and have a sense of inferiority within themselves. They are sharply self-critical and their own worst enemies in many ways. They must find a way to let themselves dream without the constant stream of Virgo's self-criticism.

☆ ☆ ☆

The descriptions of the 12 Rising signs in Part 2 of this book gave the basic nature of those signs; but knowing the Sun sign also tells us a little more, and after reading the appropriate section in this last part of the book, you can expand your knowledge of the details of personality of the Rising signs. The basics aren't altered, but the emphases on certain factors may be; the Sun sign emphasizes certain parts of the Rising sign pattern of personality when you consider the two together. Obviously, an astrologer with a full horoscope, knowing the position of Sun, Moon, and the eight planets can give you more detail still – but of any single factor in the horoscope, the Rising sign always gives more information than any other. Hopefully, I've shown you why this is – and certain things about your own personality, and the personalities of others, may be clearer for knowing about the 12 Rising signs!

TABLE 1

Latitudes and longitudes of major cities

N, E, S and W are abbreviations for the compass points. All figures are given to the nearest degree, the ° sign being omitted (so 54N, for example, means 54 degrees north) – except when a city is located on the equator (0° of latitude) or on the Greenwich longitude (0° of longitude).

Not all major cities in the countries listed are tabulated for reasons of space – what has been done is to give latitudes and longitudes for many major cities within each country, which are fairly widely spread out around the country. In this way, readers will certainly be able to find a city in the list relatively close to their birthplace.

United Kingdom & Eire	
Aberdeen	57N 3W
Belfast	55N 6W
Birmingham	52N 2W
Bristol	51N 3W
Cardiff	51N 3W
Cork	52N 8W
Donegal	55N 8W
Dublin	53N 6W
Dundalk	54N 7W
Edinburgh	56N 3W
Galway	53N 9W
Glasgow	56N 4W
Leeds	54N 2W
Limerick	53N 9W
Liverpool	53N 3W
London	52N 0°
Londonderry	55N 7W
Manchester	54N 2W
Perth	56N 3W

United Kingdom & Eire *cont.*	
Plymouth	50N 4W
Sligo	54N 9W
Southampton	51N 1W
Waterford	52N 7W

Western Europe *(including Greece and Turkey)*	
Adana	37N 35E
Alicante	38N 1W
Amiens	50N 2E
Amsterdam	52N 5E
Ankara	40N 33E
Antwerp	51N 4E
Arnhem	52N 6E
Athens	38N 23E
Balikesir	40N 28E
Barcelona	41N 2E
Bari	41N 17E
Basel	48N 8E

Western Europe *cont.*

Bayonne	44N 1W
Belfort	48N 7E
Berlin	52N 13E
Bilbao	43N 3E
Bologna	45N 11E
Bolzano	47N 11E
Bonn	51N 7E
Boulogne	51N 2E
Braga	42N 9W
Bragança (Portugal)	42N 7W
Braunschweig	52N 10E
Breda	52N 5E
Bremen	48N 9E
Brest	48N 5E
Brussels	51N 4E
Bursa	40N 29E
Cadiz	37N 6W
Cartagena	38N 1W
Catanzaro	39N 17E
Cordoba	38N 5W
Darmstadt	50N 9E
Dieppe	50N 1E
Dusseldorf	51N 7E
Erzurum	40N 41E
Essen	51N 7E
Faro	37N 8W
Florence	44N 11E
Foggia	41N 16E
Frankfurt	50N 9E
Freiburg (Baden)	48N 8E
Geneva	46N 7E
Genoa	44N 8E
Gerona	42N 3E
Ghent	51N 4E
Gibraltar	36N 5W
Graz	47N 15E
Guarda	40N 7W
Hanover	52N 10E
Innsbruck	47N 11E
Istanbul	41N 29E
Izmir	38N 27E
Karlsruhe	49N 8E
Kavalla	41N 24E
Koblenz	50N 8E
Lausanne	47N 7E
Le Havre	50N 0°

Western Europe *cont.*

Lerida	42N 1E
Limoges	46N 1E
Linz (Austria)	48N 14E
Lisbon	39N 9W
Lucerne	47N 8E
Luxembourg	50N 7E
Lyon	46N 5E
Madrid	40N 4W
Majorca	40N 3E
Mannheim	49N 8E
Marseilles	43N 5E
Messina	38N 16E
Milan	45N 9E
Montpelier	44N 4E
Munich	48N 12E
Murcia	38N 1W
Naples	41N 14E
Nice	44N 7E
Nuremburg	49N 11E
Palencia	42N 5W
Palermo	38N 13E
Paris	49N 2E
Parma	45N 10E
Pisa	44N 10E
Porto	41N 9W
Regensburg	49N 12E
Reims	49N 4E
Rochefort	46N 1E
Rotterdam	52N 5E
Rouen	49N 1E
St Etienne	45N 4E
Salonika	41N 23E
San Marino	44N 12E
Seville	37N 6W
Strasbourg	49N 8E
Stuttgart	49N 9E
Taranto	41N 17E
Toledo	40N 4W
Toulouse	44N 1E
Trikkala	40N 22E
Turin	45N 8E
Utrecht	52N 5E
Venice	45N 12E
Versailles	49N 2E
Vienna	48N 16E
Wurzberg	50N 10E

Western Europe *cont.*

Xanthi	41N 25E
Zurich	47N 9E

Scandinavia

Aarhus	58N 10E
Bergen	60N 5E
Copenhagen	56N 13E
Gothenburg	58N 12E
Halsingborg	56N 13E
Helsinki	60N 25E
Malmo	56N 13E
Norrkoping	59N 16E
Odense	55N 10E
Oslo	60N 11E
Reykjavik	64N 22W
Stavanger	59N 6E
Stockholm	59N 18E
Tampere	62N 24E
Tromso	70N 19E
Trondheim	63N 10E
Uppsala	60N 18E
Vesteralen	69N 15E

Central & Southern America

Antofagasta	24S 71W
Arequipa	16S 72W
Arica (Chile)	19S 70W
Asuncion (Paraguay)	25S 57W
Bahia Blanca	39S 62W
Belem	1S 49W
Belize City	17N 88W
Belo Horizonte	20S 44W
Bogota	5N 74W
Brasilia	10S 69W
Buenos Aries	35S 58W
Cali	3N 77W
Callao (Peru)	12S 77W
Caracas	11N 67W
Cayenne	5N 52W
Cochabamba	17S 66W
Comodoro Rivadavia	46S 68W
Concepcion (Bolivia)	16S 62W
Concepcion (Chile)	37S 73W
Concepcion (Paraguay)	24S 57W
Cuiaba	16S 56W
Curitiba	25S 49W

Central & Southern America *cont.*

Cuzco	14S 72W
Fortaleza	4S 39W
Georgetown	7N 58W
Guadalajara	21N 103W
Guatemala City	15N 90W
Guayaquil	2S 80W
Havana	23N 82W
Iquique	20S 70W
Iquitos	4S 73W
Kingston (Jamaica)	18N 77W
La Paz (Bolivia)	16S 68W
La Paz (Honduras)	14N 88W
La Paz (Venezuela)	11N 72W
La Plata	35S 58W
Leon (Nicaragua)	12N 87W
Lima	12S 77W
Managua	12N 87W
Medellin	6N 76W
Mendoza	33S 69W
Merida (Mexico)	21N 90W
Merida (Venezuela)	9N 71W
Mexico City	19N 99W
Montevideo	35S 56W
Panama	9N 79W
Paysandu	32S 58W
Port au Prince	19N 72W
Porto Alegre (Rio Grande, Brazil)	30S 57W
Puebla	19N 98W
Recife	8S 35W
Rio de Janeiro	23S 43W
San Jose (Costa Rica)	10N 84W
San Juan (Puerto Rico)	18N 66W
Santiago (Chile)	33S 71W
Santiago de Cuba	20N 76W
Santo Domingo	19N 70W
Santos	24S 46W
Sao Luis	3S 44W
Sao Paulo	24S 47W
Sucre	19S 65W
Talara	5S 81W
Torreon	26N 103W
Valdivia	40S 73W
Valparaiso (Chile)	33S 71W
Vera Cruz	19N 96W
Vina del Mar	33S 72W

Canada

Battle Harbour	52N 56W
Brandon	50N 100W
Calgary	51N 114W
Churchill	59N 95W
Coppermine	68N 116W
Edmonton	54N 114W
Fort Chima	58N 68W
Fort Nelson	59N 123W
Fort Providence	61N 118W
Fort Smith	60N 112W
Fort Vermillion	58N 116W
Goose Bay	53N 60W
Halifax	45N 64W
Hay River	61N 116W
McMurray	57N 111W
Montreal	46N 74W
Norman Wells	66N 128W
North Battleford	53N 108W
Ottawa	45N 76W
Peace River	56N 117W
Prince Albert	53N 106W
Regina	51N 105W
St. John's	48N 53W
Saskatoon	52N 107W
Sault Ste Marie	47N 84W
Schefferville	55N 67W
Sudbury	47N 81W
Toronto	44N 79W
Vancouver	49N 123W
Winnipeg	50N 97W
Yellowknife	63N 114W

United States of America

Atlanta	34N 84W
Baltimore	39N 77W
Boston	42N 71W
Chicago	42N 88W
Dallas (Texas)	33N 97W
Denver	40N 105W
Detroit	42N 83W
Fort Worth	33N 97W
Greensboro (NC)	36N 79W
Houston (Texas)	30N 95W
Jacksonville (Fl)	30N 82W
Kansas City	39N 95W
Los Angeles	34N 118W

United States of America *cont.*

Louisville (Ken)	38N 85W
Memphis	35N 90W
Milwaukee	43N 88W
Minneapolis	46N 93W
New Orleans	30N 90W
New York	41N 74W
Norfolk (Va)	37N 76W
Oklahoma City	35N 98W
Peoria (Ill)	41N 90W
Phoenix (Ariz)	34N 112W
Portland (Mich)	43N 85W
Sacramento	39N 121W
San Antonio (Texas)	30N 99W
San Diego (Ca)	33N 117W
San Francisco	38N 123W
San Jose (Ca)	37N 122W
Seattle	48N 112W
Syracuse	43N 76W
Washington (DC)	39N 77W

Australia & New Zealand

Adelaide	36S 139E
Albany	35S 113E
Alice Springs	24S 134E
Auckland	37S 175E
Brisbane	27S 153E
Bundaberg	25S 152E
Cairns	17S 146E
Canberra	35S 149E
Carnarvon (W. Aus)	25S 114E
Christchurch	44S 173E
Darwin	12S 131E
Dunedin	46S 171E
Geelong	38S 144E
Geraldton (W. Aus)	29S 114E
Hamilton	38S 175E
Invercargill	46S 138E
Kalgoorlie	31S 121E
Melbourne	38S 145E
Napier	40S 177E
Nelson	41S 173E
Newcastle	33S 152E
Perth	32S 116E
Port Pirie	33S 136E
Queenstown	45S 169E
Rockhampton	23S 151E

Australia & New Zealand *cont.*	
Townsville	19S 147E
Wanganui	40S 175E
Wellington	41S 174E

Indian subcontinent	
Agra	27N 78E
Ahmadabad	23N 73E
Allahabad	26N 82E
Bangalore	13N 75E
Bareilly	28N 79E
Baroda	26N 77E
Benares	25N 83E
Bombay	19N 73E
Calcutta	23N 88E
Cocanada	17N 82E
Colombo	7N 80E
Cuttack	20N 86E
Dacca	24N 90E
Delhi	29N 77E
Hyderabad (India)	17N 78E
Hyderabad (Pakistan)	25N 69E
Jabalpur	23N 80E
Jaffna	10N 80E
Jaipur	27N 73E
Jamshedpur	23N 86E
Jodhpur	26N 73E
Kandi	24N 88E
Kanpur	27N 80E
Karachi	25N 67E
Lahore	31N 74E
Lucknow	27N 81E
Madras	13N 80E
Madurai	10N 78E
Mangalore	13N 75E
Mysore	13N 77E
Nagpur	21N 79E
Palanpur	24N 72E
Panjim	16N 74E
Patna	24N 85E
Peshawar	34N 72E
Poona	18N 74E
Quetta	30N 67E
Raipur	21N 82E
Ratnagiri	17N 73E
Sambalpur	21N 84E
Scholapur	17N 77E

Indian subcontinent *cont.*	
Trivandrum	9N 77E

Japan & South-East Asia	
Bali	8S 115E
Bangka (Sumatra)	2S 106E
Bangkok	14S 101E
Brunei	5N 115E
Chanthaburi	13N 102E
Chon Buri	13N 101E
Dagupan	16N 121E
Davao	7N 125E
Dipolog	9N 124E
Dulawan	7N 124E
Fukuoka	34N 131E
George Town (Malaysia)	5N 100E
Gifu	36N 137E
Hamamatsu	35N 138E
Hong Kong	22N 114E
Ipuh	3S 101E
Jakarta	8S 110E
Kagoshima	32N 131E
Kanazawa	37N 137E
Kobe	35N 135E
Kochi	34N 134E
Korat	15N 102E
Kota Bharu	6N 102E
Kuala Lumpur	3N 101E
Kuching	2N 110E
Kumamoto	33N 131E
Kushiro	43N 145E
Kyoto	35N 136E
Laoag	18N 121E
Luzon	17N 122E
Mandalay	22N 96E
Manila	14N 120E
Matsumoto	36N 138E
Matsuyama	34N 133E
Medan	4N 99E
Mindanao	8N 125E
Miyazaki	32N 132E
Moulmein	17N 98E
Muang Nan	19N 101E
Muang Ubon	15N 105E
Myingyan	22N 96E
Nagano	37N 138E

Japan & South-East Asia *cont.*

Nagasaki	33N 130E
Nagoya	35N 137E
Niigata	38N 139E
Omuta	33N 131E
Palembang	3S 105E
Quezon City	15N 121E
Rangoon	17N 96E
Rat Buri	14N 100E
Samar	12N 125E
Sapporo	43N 142E

Japan & South-East Asia *cont.*

Shizuoka	35N 139E
Singapore	1N 104E
Surabaja	7S 113E
Taipei	25N 122E
Thayetmyo	20N 96E
Tokyo	35N 140E
Tsuyama	35N 134E
Yamaguchi	34N 132E
Yamethin	21N 96E
Zamboanga	7N 122E

TABLE 2

Time zones

Differences between local time and GMT are given here for many major countries of the world.

(I) Local time earlier than GMT

The number of hours difference is given; when correcting to GMT, *add* the number of hours to the local birth time to find the GMT at the moment of birth.

Antigua	4	Guatemala	6
Argentina	3	Guyana	3
Barbados	4	Haiti	5
Brazil	3	Honduras	6
Canada	see below	Jamaica	5
Chile	4	Mexico	6
Colombia	5	Nicaragua	6
Costa Rica	6	Panama	5
Cuba	5	Peru	5
Dominican Republic	4	Trinidad & Tobago	4
Ecuador	5	United States	see below
El Salvador	6	Uruguay	3
Grenada	4	Venezuela	4

Note: Canada has various times zones, with local times $3\frac{1}{2}$ to 9 hours behind GMT; the United States has various times zones with local times 5 to 11 hours behind GMT. Telephone companies and local libraries can inform you as to the exact time difference from GMT for a specific area within Canada or the US.

(II) Local time the same as GMT

The following countries have no difference between their local time and GMT, so a local-time birth time is the same as birth time in GMT. These countries are: Ghana, Iceland, Ivory Coast, Liberia, Niger and Portugal.

(III) Local time later than GMT

The number of hours difference is given; when correcting to GMT, *subtract* the number of hours from the local birth time to find the GMT at the moment of birth.

Algeria	1	Malysia	see below
Angola	1	Morocco	1
Australia	see below	Mozambique	2
Austria	1	Netherlands	1
Bangaladesh	6	New Zealand	12
Belgium	1	Nigeria	1
Botswana	2	Norway	1
Burma	$6\frac{1}{2}$	Pakistan	5
Cyprus	2	Philippines	8
Denmark	1	San Marino	1
Egypt	2	Singapore	9
Ethiopia	3	Somalia	3
Fiji	12	South Africa	2
Finland	2	Spain	1
France	1	Sri Lanka	$5\frac{1}{2}$
West Germany	1	Sudan	2
Gibraltar	1	Sweden	1
Greece	2	Switzerland	1
Hong Kong	8	Taiwan	8
India	$5\frac{1}{2}$	Tanzania	3
Indonesia	see below	Thailand	7
Italy	1	Tunisia	1
Japan	9	Turkey	3
Kenya	3	Uganda	3
Libya	2	Zambia	2
Luxembourg	1	Zimbabwe	2
Malawi	2		

Note: Australia (8 to 10 hours difference) and Indonesia (7 to 9 hours difference) have multiple time zones and Malaysia ($7\frac{1}{2}$ or 8 hours difference) has two. Telephone companies and local libraries can inform you as to the exact time difference from GMT for a specific area within each country.

TABLE 3

British Summer Time

British Summer Time has been kept for all years since 1916. Beginning at 02.00 GMT on the earlier of the two dates given for each year, and ending at 02.00 GMT (03.00 BST) on the later date, BST is in force. If your birth time falls during the period of time when BST is in operation, *subtract* one hour to get your birth time in GMT, except for years marked with an asterisk (*)—for these years, when Double Summer Time was in effect, subtract *two hours*.

	BST starts	BST ends		BST starts	BST ends
1916	21 May	1 Oct	1937	18 April	3 Oct
1917	8 April	17 Sept	1938	10 April	2 Oct
1918	24 March	30 Sept	1939	16 April	19 Nov
1919	30 March	29 Sept	1940	25 Feb	31 Dec
1920	28 March	25 Oct	1941*	1 Jan	31 Dec
1921	3 April	3 Oct	1942*	1 Jan	31 Dec
1922	26 March	8 Oct	1943*	1 Jan	31 Dec
1923	22 April	16 Sept	1944*	1 Jan	31 Dec
1924	13 April	21 Sept	1945*	1 Jan	31 Dec
1925	19 April	4 Oct	1946	14 April	6 Oct
1926	18 April	3 Oct	1947	16 March	2 Nov
1927	10 April	2 Oct	1948	14 March	31 Oct
1928	22 April	7 Oct	1949	3 April	30 Oct
1929	21 April	6 Oct	1950	16 April	22 Oct
1930	13 April	5 Oct	1951	15 April	21 Oct
1931	19 April	4 Oct	1952	20 April	26 Oct
1932	17 April	2 Oct	1953	19 April	4 Oct
1933	9 April	8 Oct	1954	11 April	3 Oct
1934	22 April	7 Oct	1955	17 April	2 Oct
1935	14 April	6 Oct	1956	22 April	7 Oct
1936	19 April	4 Oct	1957	14 April	6 Oct

	BST starts	BST ends		BST starts	BST ends
1958	20 April	5 Oct	1972	19 March	29 Oct
1959	19 April	4 Oct	1973	18 March	28 Oct
1960	10 April	2 Oct	1974	17 March	27 Oct
1961	26 March	29 Oct	1975	16 March	26 Oct
1962	25 March	28 Oct	1976	21 March	24 Oct
1963	31 March	27 Oct	1977	20 March	23 Oct
1964	22 March	25 Oct	1978	19 March	29 Oct
1965	21 March	24 Oct	1979	18 March	28 Oct
1966	20 March	23 Oct	1980	16 March	26 Oct
1967	19 March	29 Oct	1981	29 March	25 Oct
1968	18 Feb	31 Dec	1982	28 March	24 Oct
1969	1 Jan	31 Dec	1983	27 March	23 Oct
1970	1 Jan	31 Dec	1984	25 March	28 Oct
1971	1 Jan	31 Oct	1985	31 March	27 Oct

TABLE 4

Converting GMT to Sidereal Time

Date	Jan	Feb	March	April	May	June
1	18.43	20.45	22.36	00.39	02.37	04.39
2	18.47	20.49	22.40	00.43	02.41	04.43
3	18.51	20.53	22.44	00.47	02.45	04.47
4	18.54	20.57	22.48	00.51	02.49	04.51
5	18.58	21.01	22.52	00.54	02.52	04.55
6	19.02	21.05	22.56	00.58	02.56	04.59
7	19.06	21.09	23.00	01.02	03.00	05.03
8	19.10	21.12	23.04	01.06	03.04	05.07
9	19.14	21.16	23.08	01.10	03.08	05.11
10	19.18	21.20	23.12	01.14	03.12	05.15
11	19.22	21.24	23.16	01.18	03.16	05.18
12	19.26	21.28	23.20	01.22	03.20	05.22
13	19.30	21.32	23.24	01.26	03.24	05.26
14	19.34	21.36	23.28	01.30	03.28	05.30
15	19.38	21.40	23.32	01.34	03.32	05.34
16	19.42	21.44	23.36	01.38	03.36	05.38
17	19.46	21.48	23.40	01.42	03.40	05.42
18	19.50	21.52	23.44	01.46	03.44	05.46
19	19.54	21.56	23.48	01.50	03.48	05.50
20	19.58	22.00	23.52	01.54	03.52	05.54
21	20.01	22.04	23.56	01.57	03.56	05.58
22	20.05	22.08	24.00	02.01	03.59	06.02
23	20.09	22.12	00.04	02.05	04.03	06.06
24	20.13	22.16	00.07	02.09	04.07	06.10
25	20.17	22.19	00.11	02.13	04.11	06.14
26	20.21	22.23	00.15	02.17	04.15	06.17
27	20.25	22.27	00.19	02.21	04.19	06.21
28	20.29	22.31	00.23	02.25	04.23	06.25
29	20.33	22.34	00.27	02.29	04.27	06.29
30	20.37		00.31	02.33	04.31	06.33
31	20.41		00.35		04.35	

Using this table: Check on the table below the Sidereal Time given for the date of your birth (the year doesn't matter). This time is the Sidereal Time at NOON GMT. If your birth was *before* noon GMT, *subtract* the difference between your birth time and noon from the Sidereal Time. If your birth was *after* noon GMT, *add* the difference between your birth time and noon to the Sidereal Time. If adding this difference gives a figure exceeding 24 hours for Sidereal Time, simply subtract 24 hours from the figure you get — and likewise, if you get a figure below zero hours add 24 hours to it.

Example: A person born at 7.20 (a.m.) GMT on May 1 should calculate a Sidereal Time for their birth of 02.37 (from the table) minus 4 hours and 40 minutes (difference between birth time and noon GMT), giving a Sidereal Time of minus 2 hours and 3 minutes. Adding 24 hours to bring this above zero gives the correct Sidereal Time of 21.57.

Date	July	Aug	Sept	Oct	Nov	Dec
1	06.37	08.40	10.42	12.40	14.42	16.41
2	06.41	08.44	10.46	12.44	14.46	16.44
3	06.45	08.48	10.50	12.48	14.50	16.48
4	06.49	08.52	10.54	12.52	14.54	16.52
5	06.53	08.56	10.58	12.56	14.58	16.56
6	06.57	08.59	11.02	13.00	15.02	17.00
7	07.01	09.03	11.06	13.04	15.06	17.04
8	07.05	09.07	11.10	13.08	15.10	17.08
9	07.09	09.11	11.14	13.12	15.14	17.12
10	07.13	09.15	11.18	13.16	15.18	17.16
11	07.17	09.19	11.22	13.20	15.22	17.20
12	07.21	09.23	11.26	13.23	15.26	17.24
13	07.25	09.27	11.29	13.27	15.30	17.28
14	07.29	09.31	11.33	13.31	15.33	17.32
15	07.33	09.35	11.37	13.35	15.37	17.36
16	07.37	09.39	11.41	13.39	15.41	17.40
17	07.41	09.43	11.45	13.43	15.45	17.44
18	07.45	09.47	11.49	13.47	15.49	17.48
19	07.49	09.51	11.53	13.51	15.53	17.52
20	07.53	09.55	11.57	13.55	15.57	17.55
21	07.57	09.59	12.01	13.59	16.01	17.59
22	08.00	10.02	12.05	14.03	16.05	18.03
23	08.04	10.06	12.09	14.07	16.09	18.07
24	08.08	10.10	12.13	14.11	16.13	18.11
25	08.12	10.14	12.16	14.15	16.17	18.15
26	08.16	10.18	12.20	14.18	16.21	18.19
27	08.20	10.22	12.24	14.22	16.25	18.23
28	08.24	10.26	12.28	14.26	16.29	18.27
29	08.28	10.30	12.32	14.30	16.33	18.31
30	08.32	10.34	12.36	14.34	16.37	18.35
31	08.36	10.38		14.38		18.39

TABLE 5

Computing your Rising sign

Using this table: This table gives the Rising sign for different Sidereal Times for latitudes from 2° to 60° north of the equator. For each latitude, the Sidereal Time (using a 24-hour clock) at which the signs begin to 'rise' over the horizon is given. Knowing the Sidereal Time when you were born, check the Rising sign – using the right latitude! If you do not know the exact latitude of the place where you were born, Table 1 contains the latitudes for a large number of major cities – use the latitude of a major city close to where you were born.

The latitudes in the table are given at 2° intervals – use the closest one to the exact latitude for your birthplace. So, if the birthplace was (say) London, which is 51½°N, use the 52° table.

When you know the right latitude table, simply check which interval your birth time falls in – for example, someone born at 52°N latitude at a Sidereal Time of 10.15 would have Scorpio rising, since this sign 'rises' at 08.52 and 'sets' at 11.43.

	Aries	Taurus	Gemini	Cancer	Leo	Virgo	Libra	Scorpio	Sagittarius	Capricorn	Aquarius	Pisces
2°	18.00	19.49	21.48	23.57	02.06	04.06	06.00	07.53	09.54	12.03	14.12	16.10
4°	18.00	19.49	21.45	23.53	02.03	04.05	06.00	07.55	09.57	12.07	14.15	16.11
6°	18.00	19.47	21.42	23.50	02.00	04.03	06.00	07.57	10.00	12.10	14.17	16.13
8°	18.00	19.45	21.39	23.46	01.57	04.02	06.00	07.58	10.03	12.14	14.20	16.15
10°	18.00	19.43	21.36	23.43	01.53	04.00	06.00	08.00	10.06	12.18	14.23	16.17
12°	18.00	19.42	21.33	23.39	01.51	03.58	06.00	08.02	10.09	12.21	14.27	16.19
14°	18.00	19.40	21.30	23.35	01.48	03.57	06.00	08.03	10.12	12.25	14.30	16.21
16°	18.00	19.38	21.27	23.31	01.45	03.55	06.00	08.05	10.15	12.29	14.33	16.22
18°	18.00	19.37	21.24	23.27	01.41	03.53	06.00	08.07	10.18	12.33	14.36	16.24
20°	18.00	19.35	21.20	23.24	01.38	03.51	06.00	08.09	10.21	12.36	14.40	16.25
22°	18.00	19.33	21.17	23.20	01.35	03.47	06.00	08.10	10.26	12.40	14.43	16.27
24°	18.00	19.30	21.13	23.15	01.31	03.47	06.00	08.12	10.30	12.45	14.47	16.29
26°	18.00	19.28	21.09	23.11	01.27	03.45	06.00	08.14	10.33	12.49	14.50	16.31
28°	18.00	19.26	21.07	23.06	01.23	03.43	06.00	08.16	10.36	12.53	14.53	16.33
30°	18.00	19.24	21.02	23.02	01.20	03.41	06.00	08.18	10.40	12.58	14.58	16.35
32°	18.00	19.23	20.59	22.58	01.16	03.39	06.00	08.21	10.44	13.02	15.01	16.37
34°	18.00	19.21	20.54	22.52	01.12	03.36	06.00	08.23	10.48	13.08	15.06	16.39
36°	18.00	19.18	20.50	22.48	01.08	03.34	06.00	08.25	10.52	13.13	15.10	16.42
38°	18.00	19.16	20.45	22.41	01.02	03.32	06.00	08.28	10.58	13.19	15.15	16.45
40°	18.00	19.12	20.40	22.35	00.58	03.30	06.00	08.30	11.03	13.25	15.20	16.47
42°	18.00	19.10	20.34	22.28	00.52	03.26	06.00	08.34	11.08	13.32	15.25	16.50
44°	18.00	19.07	20.29	22.22	00.47	03.23	06.00	08.37	11.14	13.38	15.31	16.52
46°	18.00	19.02	20.21	22.12	00.39	03.20	06.00	08.40	11.22	13.47	15.40	16.57
48°	18.00	18.59	20.14	22.03	00.32	03.17	06.00	08.44	11.29	13.56	15.46	17.01
50°	18.00	18.55	20.07	21.55	00.25	03.13	06.00	08.47	11.35	14.05	15.53	17.05
52°	18.00	18.51	20.00	21.45	00.17	03.08	06.00	08.52	11.43	14.15	16.00	17.09
54°	18.00	18.47	19.50	21.34	00.08	03.04	06.00	08.56	11.52	14.26	16.10	17.13
56°	18.00	18.42	19.40	21.20	23.57	02.58	06.00	09.02	12.03	14.39	16.19	17.18
58°	18.00	18.36	19.28	21.02	23.44	02.52	06.00	09.08	12.15	14.57	16.33	17.24
60°	18.00	18.30	19.14	20.46	23.31	02.46	06.00	09.14	12.29	15.14	16.46	17.30

Index